insider's guide

□□□□□

www.itchysheffield.co.uk

© itchy Ltd
Globe Quay Globe Road Leeds LS11 5QG
t: 0113 246 0440 f: 0113 246 0550 e: all@itchymedia.co.uk
ISBN: 1-903753-26-0

City Editors	John Emmerson, Gayle Hetherington
Editors	Simon Gray, Mike Waugh, Andrew Wood
Design	Matt Wood, Chris McNamara
Photography	Philippa Black
Contributors	Rachel Boughton, Emma Bradley, Eve Burton, Michael Cresswell, Alex Donohoe, Alice Elliot, Neil Fairchild, Julie Guy, Emma Herring, Robyn Johnson, Claire Millington, Jonathan Mills, Mark Pickering, Mandy Pike, Alison Swann, Rachel Taylor
Acknowledgements	Matt Alford, Emma Johnson, Susanna Mountcastle, Tallulah Thompson

contents

top fives

Oh my God we're good to you...

Not only do we write funky little books but we also offer you, the discerning entertainment junkie, some pretty fine stuff on-line.

Point your browser to **www.itchycity.co.uk** and we'll not only keep you entertained with stories and reviews about what's going on in your city, we can also send you regular emails and SMS messages about the stuff you're into. So, we'll keep you informed about where the best happy hours are, when Oakenfold's next in town or where you can find a kebab at 2am. There's also a chance for you to contribute your views and reviews and get free stuff in return (we are too good to you). Have a shoofty. Go on.

itchy box set

Oh, imagine. **All 16 titles**, an encyclopaedia of entertainment across the country, all wrapped up in a glorious multi-coloured special box. Every title below in one mother of a box. Limited edition, naturally, and so exclusive, we don't even know what it looks like ourselves.

Artist's impression. Is this what the box will look like?

If you were to buy these individually, it'd cost you a bargainous £44. But hello, what's this? We're doing the full caboodle **for a mere £35**, including free postage and packing. **Call 0113 246 0440** and order by credit/debit card and we'll whizz one over to you.

bath birmingham brighton bristol cambridge cardiff edinburgh glasgow leeds liverpool london manchester nottingham oxford sheffield york

YOU'RE IN AN INTERVIEW

sheffield 2002

"By 'eck it's grim up North". Which ever southern jessie said that certainly didn't know what they were talking about. After a year of telling you what's what, itchy Sheffield returns to give it to you in the ear again, mouthing off about where to go and what you need to know. It's just as well really, what

with loads of new bars, shops, restaurants and clubs opening all the time, if you turn your back for two minutes chances are someone will have built a café bar on your whippet. Fortunately your spankingly new and updated itchy guide can steer you through all the manic mayhem going off in the entertainment capital of Yorkshire.

It's been a year of ups and downs for Sheff. In sport both the Owls and the Blades tried their hardest to get into the 2nd Division, but true to form they both managed to mess this up at the last minute, and now you can catch two cracking Sheffield derbies a season. More

encouragingly though, the Sheffield Steelers stole the show with a grand slam winning season, and provided great entertainment and plenty of blood on the ice along the way.

On the clubbing front, The Republic had its collar felt by Johnny Law, but are up and running again; Unit shut down for an extended refurb leaving NY Sushi temporarily homeless, but they're now fully part of the furniture at Mojo's; and yes just in case you were wondering, the National Centre for Popular Music still isn't open. Not that anyone really cares, as the fab Brown Street bar and club opened up opposite, giving Sheffield revellers a pretty good alternative to going to Bed, or indeed going to bed.

On the drinking front, there were new appearances by Sola, Casa, Lounge, Ha Ha, Bar Ice and Bar Matrix, all knocking out tasty booze, and giving Sheff drinkers another good reason to get their glad rags on. Luckily, there's still plenty of places to get your threads too, as The Forum still provides some quality cool clothing.

With loads of new cool and groovy stuff to do, plus a few old favourites too, if you don't absolutely love it in Sheff you're obviously just stupid, inbred, or from Kendray (sorry is there a difference?). Steel yourself for a bumpy ride.

DON'T GET INTIMIDATED BY THEIR EYE CONTACT

■ ■ Two Hours

Right, loads to do, but not much time. Start off with a quick coffee in **The Showroom Café**, or some might prefer a couple of quick shooters in **Brown Street** opposite. Neck these down and then head up to Devonshire Street to check out **The Forum** which has a dazzling array of funky fashions and groovy gear. Then pop across the road for a well deserved drink in **The Frog & Parrot**, they have many great beers, but only have one as time is pressing. Stick your head round the door in **Con Brio** and listen to a few great sounds from their extensive world music collection. If you've got time pop up West Street and grab some chips in **The Lounge**, and then maybe toss a frisbee about in the **Botanical Gardens**. After that your time will probably be up, but you've been treated to a great snapshot of this fantastic city.

■ ■ Two Days

Stay – You really gotta get a room at **The Hotel Bristol**. Not only is it the coolest and most interesting hotel in the city, at the

weekends it's a mere £49.50 for a double room – although you can comfortably sleep three people in each room, and they don't mind either – quite handy if you get really lucky in **Po Na Na**. Breakfast is an additional £8.50 for a Full English or £6.50 for a continental. That'll be a Full English then.

Shop – Your best bet is to check out **The Forum** on Devonshire Street for loads of funky and alternative shops all under one roof. Alternatively if you want to give your plastic the beating of its life, hop on the tram to **Meadowhall**. With thousands of high street names all within the same square mile, it can be a bit dull, but that doesn't stop the hordes packing the place out every weekend.

Attractions – For a bit of culture have a look at **The Graves Art Gallery** with an exceptional collection of exhibits including etchings, photography, and sculptures. There's also **The Site Gallery** with extensive exhibits dedicated to photography and different forms of visual media. Give your peepers a treat at **The Showroom Cinema** which shows some of the best classic films you're ever likely to catch on the silver screen. Alternatively you could catch a play

"OI, WHAT ARE YOU LOT STARING AT!?"

2hours2days2hours2days2hours2days2hours2days **2hours2days**

at **The Crucible**, or watch "Rocket" Ronnie pot the pink when they hold the annual snooker championships here. If all that culture has made you feel giddy, have a pint at **The Kelham Island** brewery opposite the fantastic **Fat Cat** pub. Or you could take an indie pilgrimage to **The Washington**, it's where Pulp were formed, and a damn fine boozer too.

Drink – Vodka? Too bloody right. Head to **Revolution** which has an astonishing array

of the white stuff. Stumbling out of there you could catch some chilled out grooves at **Sola** bar, or see some DJs spinning a few discs at **The Forum Cafe** or just next door at **The Halcyon Bar** – this is a great venue to fire up your weekend. If you want a bit more of a traditional pub experience **The Frog & Parrot** will sort you out with a great selection of real ales, plus its own super strength homebrew, or there's **The Porter Cottage** which is probably the best pub in the city – check it out to see why.

Eat – For classy and innovative English cooking there's the fab and highly acclaimed **Rafters** restaurant. Alternatively **The Mediterranean** on Sharrow Vale Road

serves some of the best seafood in Sheff. **Bahn Nah** provides a classy and tasty take on Chinese and Oriental cuisine, or you could get your teeth into some fine African cooking at **UK Mama's** in Broomhill. Or for a full on debauched ruby, you really can't do better than taking a trip to **Balti King**, this baby knocks out cracking and cheap curries 'til 4am every morning. It's no wonder they call him the King.

Club – Where do you start? There's the fantastically glamorous **Bed** which really is the house of House. If you want to bop to hip hop and r'n'b there's nowhere finer than NY Sushi at **Mojo's**. **Unit** knocks out everything from knock out US house to some groovy funk. **The Fez Club** is one of the best small clubs in the country for its squished blissed

out sounds, and the small and sexy **Orchis** isn't far behind. **The Republic** was made world famous by Gatecrasher, but apart from that bad boy it does great nights throughout the week. Or if you fancy something a bit more alternative, take a look at **Corporation** with a fantastically diverse music policy, or there's **Casbah** for a hearty diet of rock.

BEWARE OF THE VOICES. FOR CAREER ADVICE WORTH LISTENING TO, INCLUDING **HELP** WITH **INTERVIEWS**, VISIT monster.co.uk

www.itchy**sheffield**.co.uk   7

Award winning specialists in Indian food

BILASH
Tandoori
HOUSE

est. 1986

TELEPHONE: (0114) 266 1746

10% STUDENT DISCOUNT

MONDAY - SUNDAY 5:50PM TO MIDNIGHT
FRIDAY - SATURDAY 5:30PM TO 1:00AM
347 SHARROW VALE ROAD, HUNTERS BAR
VISIT US:
WWW.BILASHTANDOORI.CO.UK

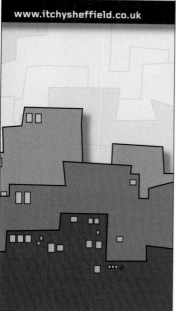

restaurants

www.itchysheffield.co.uk

■ ■ English

■ ■ Beauchief Hotel and Restaurant
161 Abbeydale Road South
(0114) 262 0500

Set in the leafy suburb of Beauchief, well out of the city centre, this restaurant is a treat not to be missed. The hotel is situated in beautiful grounds and the restaurant within, maintains the elegant standard. If you have particularly deep pockets (or if someone else is paying) you could opt for the à la carte menu with individually-priced courses. For those on a smaller budget the table d'hotel menu compares very reasonably with the major hotels in the city, and is far better than you'd expect compared to the usual turgid hotel grub.
Mon-Fri 12pm-2pm and 7pm-9.45pm.
Sat 12pm-4pm and 7pm-9.45pm
Meal for two: £50 (Fillet steak)

■ ■ Brasserie Leo
10 Sharrow Lane (0114) 258 9411

Set within a converted Victorian mansion house, it's no surprise that their accompanying restaurant is a pretty impressive affair. The menu offers delights such as 'clafoutis' and 'clotted cream chiboust', whatever that means, whilst the setting is sophisticated if a little old fashioned. The menu is dominated by traditional steak, fish and poultry dishes with all the trimmings but my girlfriend goes solely for the desert menu. One Creme Brulé and she's anyones. They put together a fantastic breakfast so it's almost worth asking your waiter for a sleeping bag whilst you wait.
Mon-Sat 6.30pm-10.30pm
Meal for two £42 (Duck Breast)

THE **AMERICAN** RESTAURANT & BAR

With over

100 mouth-watering dishes

and more than

500 delicious cocktails,

get down to T.G.I. FRIDAY'S

and experience the magic

for yourself.

SHEFFIELD

■ ■ ■ Rafters
220 Oakbrook Rd (0114) 230 4819

Founded by local lads, the Bosworth Brothers, this place has a reputation for delivering first class and inventive English style cooking. Rafters is a Michelin star restaurant which is not surprising given the imagination and exquisite delivery of most of the dishes. If you're looking for an informal, yet very refined, dining experience then look no further, no it's not cheap, but neither are you, are you?

Wed-Sat 7pm-10pm
Meal for two: £55 (Three course set menu. BYO, £3 corkage)

■ ■ ■ American

■ ■ ■ Champs
315-319 Ecclesall Road (0114) 266 6333

A true sports theme bar and restaurant with the requisite pieces of sports memorabilia. A popular choice with locals and students. The food menu offers an extensive choice and is very reasonably priced, plus the bar has an excellent range of cocktails. Whether you're eating or drinking you can watch live sport on one of the 60 TV's scattered about the place. Everyone tends to wear their glad rags in here, though it's not a flashy joint, but I suppose it's flashy for Sheffield.

Mon-Sun 12pm-10.30pm
Meal for two: £28 (Fajitas)

■ ■ ■ TGI Fridays
Sheffield Road (0114) 244 3386

A proper American diner. They do the whole burgers, steaks and ribs thing better than most others and they even throw in a few pastas and salads for the colon conscious. They've been around for decades and have just about perfected the Yank dining experience: Silly uniforms, friendly staff, wicked 'shakes and enough cocktails to make sure you never have to have the same one twice. Out on Junction 27, but it's worth the cab fare.

Mon-Sat 12pm-11.30, Sun 12pm-10.30pm
Meal for two: £40 (Rump steak)

■ ■ ■ Uncle Sam's Chuck Wagon
298 Ecclesall Road (0114) 266 8588

The burgers are beefier than Sly, the spare ribs juicier than Cameron Diaz, and the garlic bread smells like Gerard Depardieu. Its location in student central makes it a handy stop off joint after you've had a few bevvies. What occasionally lets this place down is the staff, who are either over attentive or in the middle of a black out. Not that it's a problem, I just call an ambulance and don't leave a tip. It's also worth knowing that they do very cheap and very potent cocktails on a Sunday.

Mon-Thu 12pm-11.30pm, Fri/Sat 12pm-12am, Sun 12pm-11pm
Meal for two: £22 (1/2lb Cheese burger)

■■■ French

■■■ Café Rouge
383-385 Ecclesall Road (0114) 268 2232

Like sailors, all the nice girls love a Café Rouge. This whopping chain aims at creating the myth of a 1920s Parisian bistro, but in reality it seems more like a modern day version of Allo Allo. Mind you, its success is not based upon its French je ne sais quoi, but rather its cast iron Anglo Saxon certainty that nothing will be too adventurous – all dishes are tasty; the food and wine reasonably priced, and there's not a frog's leg in sight. CR's position halfway down Ecclesall Road means that it's a fine place to stop and have a bite to eat amid a day's shopping, although whenever I go everyone in there seems to be having affairs – maybe a bit of French is rubbing off on them after all.
Mon-Sat 10am-11pm, Sun 10am-10.30pm
Meal for two: £30 (Beef Bourguignon)

■■■ Indian

■■■ Anila's & Vijays
17-21 Charter Square (0114) 272 2861
The luminous and glitzy exterior means that you'll struggle to miss this place, and true to appearance this is a curry house and a half. The Bollywood themed cocktail bar seems a bit silly, but it's also a lot of fun, and adds vibrancy and colour which you don't get with most curry houses. There's a full Indian and Balti menu ensuring that all strengths of curry are catered for, from the faint hearted Korma lovers to the hard-core curry connoisseurs. It's the sort of place for couples rather than groups of pissed-up lads, but they can take bookings for up to 120 people – so you could hold your wedding reception here.
Mon-Sun 6pm-12am
Meal for two: £24 (Chicken Bhuna).

■■■ Ayesha's
407 Ecclesall Road (0114) 266 6003
Cosy Indian on the long restaurant strip that is Ecclesall Road. It's pretty relaxed and quiet and the food is so good that it's really not fair to rock up here after a session at The Porter Brook and ruin it. Turn up sober, have a nice meal, then get nailed at any of the many watering holes on this road – it makes a lot more sense that way. Incidentally, in case you were wondering the place is named Ayesha after a chef who used to work here. (What happened to Ayesha, I hear you ask? He got out.)
Sun-Thu 6pm-12am, Fri/Sat 6pm-12.45am
Meal for two: £25 (Chicken Bhuna)

■ ■ ■ Balti King
216 Fulwood Road (0114) 266 6655

"A curry? After 15 pints? I should coco". We Brits simply can't get enough of them and whether it's in some boozed-up state or on a pleasant Saturday afternoon, Balti King is definitely the Indian restaurant to be in. With over 200 dishes to choose from, rustled up by a team of award winning chefs, this long acclaimed restaurant will leave you extremely satisfied. Better still it's the only place in Sheffield where you can get a curry at 3.30am any night of the week, and you can bet that just about all the cabbies in the city will know where it is. And if that's too much effort then the King will come to you, with free delivery on takeaways within a 3 mile radius – what could be simpler? A compulsory visit.
Mon-Sun 12pm-4am
Meal for two: £18 (Chicken Balti)

■ ■ ■ Elinas Tandoori House
282 Sharrow Vale Road (0114) 267 9846
Elinas lies patiently in wait for stumbling wrecks to wander past and decide they'd actually feel better if they sat themselves down and stuffed their faces with curry. The food is okay, and the Spar is 2 minutes away, so if you really feel the need you can bring your own wine. It's quite a small place, but this

ensures your doting attention, although why they should have to look after you in that state I don't know. If you've had a few at The Porter next door and you fancy some hearty food, then this place does the trick nicely.
Sun-Thu 5.30pm-11pm,
Fri/Sat 5.30pm-12.30am
Meal for two: £22 (Chicken Dansak)

■ ■ ■ The Himalayan
290-292 London Road (0114) 258 5050
Don't be scared by the blacked out windows – it's actually a good thing as it means you don't have to put up with passers by staring at you as you dribble curry down your chin, and in turn you can forget that you've gone for a night out in a dodgy area of London Road. The service and bar area make this feel a lot more like a restaurant than a traditional curry house. Another bonus is that the layout means you have a choice of tables dependant on the occasion – you could bring a party here and take over the place, but it also has plenty of cosy secluded spots if you want to chomp on chapattis with a loved one. Friendly staff add to the pleasant atmosphere, which basically leaves us nothing to complain about. Damn.
Sun-Thu 6pm-1am, Fri/Sat 6pm-2pm
Meal for two: £17 (Chicken Rogan Josh)

■ ■ ■ Nirmals
189-193 Glossop Road (0114) 272 4054
Recommended by the Good Food Guide, so do them a favour, go in sober and actually taste the food for once, as the extensive and creative menu is well worth it. There's also a wide selection of vegetarian options. Usually itchy recommend that you go for a ruby when completely pie eyed, but not

with this one, no siree, it's a bit of class here, and you would do well to respect that.

Mon–Sat 12.15pm-2.30pm, 6pm-12am, Sun 6pm-12am
Meal for two: £24 (Chicken Dansak)

■■■ SB's
4 Leadmill Road (0114) 275 1966

The whiff of Indian food enters your nostrils as soon as you're within 100 yards of this restaurant – you'd think they'd planted curry trees in the station car park. The restaurant is spacious and authentic, filled with Indian music and super keen waiters. Dining here isn't an intimate experience though as all and sundry can catch a glimpse of you through the very large windows. The array of exotic dishes on offer, as well as the more expensive prices means that SB's attracts the discerning curry eater rather than the pissed up student.

Mon-Thu 6pm-2.30am, Fri/Sat 6pm-3am, Sun 6pm-1am
Meal for two: £16 (Chicken Bhuna)

■■■ Italian

■■■ BB's
119 Devonshire Street (0114) 279 9394

A cracking and affordable Italian restaurant, that's a safe bet for some top pizza/pasta pigging out. It's becoming a popular spot with Sheffield's skin flint bosses for an office night out, as the B.Y.O. policy means the company can save a fortune by bringing cans of Fanta and jars of Nescafe. The surroundings aren't overly authentic, but are cosy and homely, and the staff are exceedingly friendly, even though most of them are from Barnsley rather than Bologna. There's the usual Italian dishes, plus one or two more adventurous ones and a well-stocked desert menu, so there's not much chance you'll leave hungry. And better still, seeing the food's pretty inexpensive, you can get through a hell of a lot of offie wine very cheaply. Hurrah.

Mon-Sat 6pm-10.30pm
Meal for two: £24 (Bispecca Diabolo)

■■■ Caffé Uno
631-633 Ecclesall Road (0114) 267 0565

Probably one of the best Caffé Uno's around with its open plan café bar style, that creates a very cosmopolitan atmosphere, and in turn draws in the upwardly mobile Sheffield crowd. Its location on one of the best streets in the city doesn't do it any harm either. The menu draws upon a variety of Mediterranean influences and it's a great place for an evening meal, lunch or just whiling away a couple of hours with a cup of coffee and some good company – and if they're not forthcoming there's a large selection of broadsheets. I don't need love, I've got the Financial Times.

Mon-Thu 10am-11pm, Fri/Sat 10am-12pm, Sun 11am-10.30pm
Meal for two: £26 (Salsiccie Saglioli)

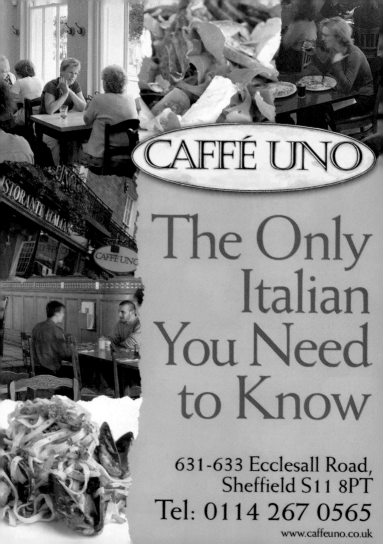

■■■ Casanova

200 Crookes (0114) 266 6684

Reasonably priced, basic Italian fare in this cosy little restaurant. Apparently those smooth Italian accents the waiting staff are sporting are all a rouse to impress the female clientele. Sadly it doesn't work – if only life was that simple, all you'd have to do to pull girls is change your name to Mario. Pity.

Mon-Thu 5.45pm-10.30pm,
Fri/Sat 5.45pm-11pm, Sun 5.45pm-10pm
Meal for two: £23 (Lasagne)

■■■ Continental Restaurant

141 West Street (0114) 279 6677

So this place is continental huh? No it's not, it's crap, and about as deeply influenced by continental cuisine as McDonald's. It's misleading claims like theirs that have made Sheffield folk scared of the Euro.

Mon-Sat 5pm-11.30pm
Meal for two: £28 (Steak Africana)

■■■ Nonna's

539-541 Ecclesall Road (0114) 268 6166

Quite unique in that virtually anything you choose on the menu is guaranteed to be delicious. Superb homemade cooking and by virtue of their adjoining delicatessen you can take back ingredients and try it yourselves at home – it may be more effort but it's a hell of a lot more interesting than buying a jar of Dolmio.

Sun-Thu 12pm-4pm and 6pm-9.45pm,
Fri/Sat 12pm-9.45pm
Meal for two: £33 (Pollo Mediterraneo)

■■■ Piccolos

3 Convent Walk (0114) 249 5040

Paper tablecloths and cheesy Italian music doesn't place Piccolos top of my list for a romantic Valentine's meal, but for a cheap and cheerful meal out then this place fits the bill. It's worth paying for a speciality dish though, as they offer huge portions and they're gorgeous. Note that the 10% student discount is only off the price of a main course – bet they don't advertise that.

Mon-Thu 5pm-11.30pm,
Fri/Sat 5pm-12am, Sun 5pm-10.30pm
Meal for two: £31 (8oz Fillet Steak)

■■■ Pizza Express

124 Devonshire Street
(0114) 275 2755

I'd been eating at this place for years before I realised it wasn't a late bar. The house wine is really good, and that's about all I remember. As with most Pizza Express restaurants it's quite attractive, inexpensive, and the food is pretty good albeit not that substantial, and the vino will get you rocking pretty quickly. For all these reasons it's a pretty good first date venue, but watch her face drop when you to try to eat your Sloppy Giuseppe pizza with extra runny egg. I can't believe I missed. Not ground breaking, but not bad either.

Mon-Sat 12pm-12am, Sun 12pm-11pm
Meal for two: £24 (Soho pizza)

■■■ Rossi's

3 Sharrow Lane (0114) 258 8164

This place should be saved for a special

LOOK AT HIM, POMPOUS IDIOT.

□ 16

itchy**sheffield** 2002

occasion, when you wish to revel in the fact that you can afford to eat here. The romantic, and surprisingly homely interior, is a perfect setting for an evening with that special person, and the delicate food lives up to all expectations.

Mon-Sat 6pm-12pm
Meal for two: £36 (Venison)

■ ■ ■ Trattoria Romana
438 Ecclesall Road (0114) 266 5491

Head out down Ecclesall Road in search of an Italian, and you won't need to look very far. However, if you're after a restaurant with a bit of class go a bit further and hunt out this little gem. It has more to offer than the predictable pizza/pasta dishes, throwing in an array of meat dishes that are swimming in mouth watering sauces. It is more expensive than some of its competitors but see this as reassuring, rather than a rip off.

Mon- Thu 5.30pm-11pm, Fri/Sat 12pm-2.30pm and 5.30-11pm, Sun 12-2.30pm and 6.30pm-10pm
Meal for two: £25 (Seafood spaghetti)

■ ■ Mexican/Spanish

■ ■ ■ K Pasa
290 Glossop Road (0114) 272 8260

Although there is a lack of Spanish restaurants in Sheffield, it doesn't make this place a godsend. Close proximity to the university, with reasonable prices means there'll always be a student, or 20, darkening its doors and licking their plate clean. Yet for those in employment or with self respect, all that awaits is a long wait, average food and sleazy waiters gawping at your boobs.

Mon-Sat 12pm-2.30pm and 5.30pm-11.30pm, Sun 6pm-10.30pm
Meal for two: £27 (Fajitas)

■ ■ ■ Viva Latino
216-218 London Road (0114) 255 3872

Really cool little Italian and Mexican themed restaurant. I'm a bit biased as they're my favourite two types of food – but why the hell does no one else actually have the talent to put dishes from different parts of the world on the same menu – it's hardly nuclear physics – and this place proves it can work. There's live music every evening and diners are invited to join in with the bands, which always seems a good idea after a couple of bottles of red, but try to stay away from the microphone, eh? If you want a different and upbeat evening out, then this is one of the best places in the city. Oh incidentally, the food is dead good too.

Mon-Sat 6pm-11pm, Sun 6pm-10.30pm
Meal for two: £21 (Tagliatelle Bandido)

■ ■ ■ Oriental

■ ■ ■ Bahn Nah
19-21 Nile Street (0114) 268 4900

Despite sounding like a noise that comes out of your mouth after one too many shandys, this is actually quite a classy joint. Although the décor is like you're in your mate's front room, the food, thank God, isn't (I'll never eat another of Mrs Gray's meat pasties if it kills me – which it probably would). Noodles, spicy and sour salads along with Thai stir fries, offer a treat for your taste buds, and can create fireworks in your mouth. Make sure you've got a beer at the ready to combat the flames, then get crack-ing sampling the delights. A surprise asset of Broomhill, and one well worth a visit.
Mon-Sat 6.30pm-11pm
Meal for two: £23 (Thai Green Curry)

■ ■ ■ Canton Orchard
377 Fulwood Road (0114) 263 0922

Nestling in a converted manor house, this grand Chinese restaurant looks and tastes fantastic. There's a very impressive array of delicious Cantonese, Pekinese and Szechuan dishes, (which as you can imagine come at a price). There's a hell of a lot of duff Chinese restaurants around, but this place is one of the better ones, so worth checking out.
Mon-Sat 5.30pm-11pm
Meal for two: £27 (Sweet & Sour Chicken)

■ ■ ■ Candy Town
27 London Road (0114) 272 5311

By far the best Chinese restaurant in Sheffield, Candy Town offers the finest meals in obvious surroundings. But it wouldn't be a Chinese without paper napkins, red lighting and chintzy wallpaper would it? And the fact it looks like the set of a dodgy European

WELL, DIGEST THIS!

porn movie should never put you off your sweet and sour. Book if you can or you'll be dissapointed. Don't say we didn't warn you.
Mon-Sat 12pm-2pm and 6pm-11.15pm,
Sun 12pm-10.30pm
Meal for two: £20 (Chicken Satay)

■ ■ Top Wok

3 Rockingham Gate (0114) 275 8838
Suspect décor should not put you off this

Sheffield classic, situated just near The Moor shopping centre. Flimsy paper copies of the University coats of arms patriotically adorn the walls, not that it makes any difference, as most students would be loyal to a cockroach if they thought they could get an NUS discount. If you're choosy about food, their 124-dish menu should sort you out.
Mon-Sat 12pm-2pm and 6pm-11.30pm
Meal for two: £22 (Sweet & Sour Chicken)

■ ■ Various

■ ■ The Bistro Casablanca

150-154 Devonshire Street
(0114) 249 0720
For over twenty years this place has been providing an unequalled service. As the

nearby bars and restaurants go for a super sleek image, Casablanca remains chilled with a very bohemian set of regulars. The interior is devoted to the Hollywood stars of the past, and unsurprisingly there are many tributes to its namesake and in respect (or maybe just to entertain) live jazz fills the air and you can drift away and imagine yourself in the company of Bogie and all the other greats of the past. They don't currently do any dishes involving a hill of beans, but it's just a matter of time.
Mon-Sun 12pm-11pm
Meal for two: £20 (Haddock)

top 5 for...	
Late Eats	
1.	Balti King
2.	SB's
3.	Vijays
4.	The Mad Greek
5.	Pizza Express

top 5 for...
Cheap Eats

1. Balti King
2. BB's
3. The Himalayan
4. Top Wok
5. Pizza Express

■■■ The Mad Greek
117 Fitzwilliam Street (0114) 272 6000

My father's advice about mad Greeks was to never play them at cards, but he never mentioned anything about their cuisine – so I investigated in a bid to discover just what made the Greek in question so mad. It can't be the food, that's pretty standard mezze and the ilk, the plate smashing's all there in abundance and the ouzo flows like water. Maybe it's because his Grandaddy promised him the finest restaurant in Yorkshire and he ended up with a mock-pillared warehouse next to a tile showroom.

Tue-Sat 7.30pm-12pm
Meal for two £30 (Swordfish)

■■■ The Mediterranean
271 Sharrow Vale Road (0114) 266 1069

The clientele here tend to be cosy couples or families out for an occasion, because this restaurant is one of Sheffield's fanciest. OK so it's not Michelin Star fancy or £50 main course fancy but the seafood menu is the best in town, and veggies get a decent selection too and that can't be said for most of the restaurants in Sheff.

Mon-Sat 12pm-2.30pm & 5.30pm-9.30pm
Meal for two: £40 (Sea bass)

■■■ UK Mama African Restaurant
257 Fulwood Road (0114) 268 7807

This was the first African restaurant in Yorkshire, and is probably still the best, it's a refreshingly original place, which offers a menu like no other. Try the Nshima with lamb and dodo to experience some of the more mysterious delights on offer. Obviously whether you rate this or slate it depends on how up for new things you are, (unless you're from Kenya, of course) but it's somewhere that needs trying. The décor's in keeping with the third world flavours served up but don't let the flakey wallpaper put you off your fufu (unless it lands in it).

Mon-Sun 5pm-2pm
Meal for two: £20 (Chicken coconut rice)

■■■ Cafés

■■■ Coffee.com
1-3 Leopold Street (0114) 270 6566

Opened at a time when sticking .com after your name automatically made you a paper millionaire and your bank manager started inviting you to golf days. They used to call themselves an internet cafe, because they had one pc, and in line with all things online going down the swanny, they've now scrapped that and it's just a coffee shop. Which isn't such a bad thing, as they've got some pretty good roasts, friendly staff, and a surprisingly un-geeky clientele.

Mon-Sat 7.45am-6.30pm

■■■ Coffee Revolution
471 Ecclesall Road (0114) 266 8565

The name above the door would lead you to believe that this place goes against the

norm. Unfortunately, there's nothing revolutionary about this place – it's yet another overpriced coffee shop with little atmosphere and individuality. Admittedly the coffee, panninis and pastries on offer are pretty good, but for the prices they charge you'd be better staying at home with your beans, a grinder and a cafetiere.
Mon-Sun 10am-10pm

■■■ Havana Internet Café
32-34 Carver Street (0114) 249 5452

Imagine my surprise upon tucking into my espresso to find that my table had been nabbed by Fidel Castro, Pablo Escobar, and Ernesto Ché Guevara all smoking fat cigars and leching menacingly at the waitresses. No? Okay it's nothing to do with Havana, but this city centre net cafe is a popular spot for stopping off for lunch and checking your e-mail. The PC service is excellent and the food is pretty good and reasonably priced. The open-plan kitchen lets you keep an eye on the chef while he rustles up your chow, and there's a healthy selection of vegetarian dishes on offer too.
Mon-Sun 10am-10pm

www.itchysheffield.co.uk

■ ■ All Bar One
13-15 Leopold Street (0114) 252 1991

All Bar One is a chain so large it's surprising B.A. Barracus isn't wearing it around his neck. Though as chain bars go it's quite pleasant; light and airy, a good wine selection and some interesting and tasty food. Usually frequented by the office beavers in the city, happily quaffing wine and trying to shag the secretary.
Mon-Sat 11.30am-11pm, Sun 12-6pm
Meal for two: £22 (Chilli pasta)

■ ■ Bar 8
29-31 Campo Lane (0114) 272 0070
Are you guilty of lugging round a musical instrument and strumming away at any available opportunity – around a campfire, in the street, round at people's houses? Yes? Then this is your heaven as you might actually find people who want to listen. Intent on nurturing the stars of tomorrow (or future dole queue devotees, depending on your charitable nature). Maybe their penchant for amateur musicians can explain why it's so quiet in here… save for the tuneless renditions of "Smoke on the Water" that is.
Mon-Sat 12-3am 7pm-11pm
Meal for two £14 (Chicken wraps)

itchy**sheffield** 2002

A MELLOW MIX OF SPIRIT AND SOUL.
THAT FLAVOURS WHATEVER IT TOUCHES.

FEEL THE

PRESENCE

TREVOR NELSON. DJ

⊕ Try it with soda and ice in a wild club.

■ ■ ■ Bar Abbey
383 Abbeydale Road (0114) 258 0414

Every effort has been made to funk up this old snooker hall, but it still looks like a hole. It's pretty isolated and doesn't look too welcoming from the outside. Inside, however, it's pretty cool with DJs spinning tracks most nights and although this is a snooker bar, the hardcore players are segregated into a "special room", so you won't have to suffer them staring at you in disdain as you feebly (and probably drunkenly) attempt to pot the black for the 20th time. It's not a bad place to while away an afternoon, the drink offers certainly cause no harm... until the next morning.

Mon-Sat 10.30am-11pm, 12pm-10.30pm
Food: Cheeseburger & chips £2.65

■ ■ ■ Bar Centro/Breez
32-34 Cambridge Street (0114) 275 8185

All office workers need to eat, and sometimes you just can't face your fifth packet sandwich of the week, which explains the popularity of Bar Centro at weekday lunchtimes. Unfortunately the club upstairs, Breez, fails to attract the same numbers of people through its doors. It remains a bit of a mystery whose business they are touting for, as the punters that fill the place in the day seem very unlikely to take advantage of the bizarre revolving dancefloor. Although if you are out on the pull, the talent in here are easier to pick up than a Boots Meal Deal – and usually cheaper as well.

Mon-Sat 10-11pm (Breez 'til 1am Fri/Sat)
Food served: Mon-Sat 10am-7pm
Meal for two: £20 (Chilli con carne)

■ ■ ■ Bar Coast
The Old Fire Station, Division Street
(0114) 279 2900

Is the seedier side of Sheffield getting you down? Pop in here and convince yourself Yorkshire's city of steel still has some style. Afternoon lounging in this chilled atmosphere can restore your faith in bar culture as you tuck into some decent food and a slightly pricey drink or two on their many ample sofas. Very popular with the beautiful people, plus one or two ugly ones and DJs liven the place up in the evenings.

Food served: 12pm-7pm
Meal for two: £17 (Stir fry chicken)

■ ■ ■ Bar Ice
16-18 Carver Street (0114) 273 8677

Hidden away just off Devonshire Street, this new bar is remarkably pretentious for Sheffield. Some might argue that they are driving the city in a more up-market direction, as that's what the hip and happening kids want. Others would just say it's poncey toss. This place isn't any great shakes; the décor's a bit trashy and most of the clientele in here are hostile old ice queens. Although having said that they do have some very comfy chairs – but then again so do dentists.

◼ ◼ Bar Matrix
Charter Square (0114) 275 4100

If you ever worry that checking your e-mail makes you look a bit geeky then this might be the answer. One of the swankiest looking bars in town which also doubles up as a huge internet café. Those who aren't here to check their Hotmail are usually checking out the hot-femail (sorry), as it's packed to the rafters with Sheff's beautiful people every

night of the week. Helped by its handy location next door to Po Na Na, and that they show The Matrix every night, guess where all the students go when they need an exit?
Mon-Sat 11-11 Sun 7pm-10.30pm
Food served 11am-7pm Mon-Sat
Food: Chicken pasta £4.90

◼ ◼ Berlin's Bar
Eyre Street (0114) 275 9469

Favoured by locals for a pint or two after work. Less than impressive surroundings cater adequately for first time drinkers, and bum fluff moustaches count as a legitimate form of ID in here. Steer clear if you've developed an aversion to boob tubes and alcopops but make it your second home if you want cheap, sickly drinks, and then fancy your chances in the "hound pound" at the nearby Uropa.
Mon/Tue 8.30pm-11.30pm, Wed/Thu 8.30pm-1am, Fri/Sat 7.30pm-1am, Sun 8pm-12.30am

◼ ◼ Brannigan's
Valley Centretainment, Broughton Lane (0114) 243 1133

Remember those girls you went to school with, who married their first boyfriend and had three kids by the time they were twenty... Well 15 years later, when hubbie Dave has run off with Tina the babysitter, those ladies, whose dreams of domestic bliss now lie in ruins, don black chiffon blouses and lycra mini skirts and cackle away, drunkenly eyeing up the Ben Sherman shirted boys who've just turned 18 whilst drowning their sorrows in Bacardi Breezers. ("Oooh have yer tried that new cranberry flavour – tastes just like Ribena – got so shit-faced on it last week I shagged my neighbour Derek, the one legged undertaker").
Mon-Thu 5.30pm-1am,
Fri/Sat 5.30pm-2am, Sun 5.30pm-10.30pm
Meal for two: £18 (Mixed grill)

■■■ Brown St
Brown Street (0114) 279 6959

A relative newcomer to the city bar scene, this bar/club is a welcome addition with its particular brand of semi-industrial chic. The place is quite stylish, with plenty of sofas for when you get bored of trying to look cool. It tends to be quiet during the day, mainly because the penny hasn't dropped with most of its regulars that it's not just a club. However, whilst this misconception persists it's worth getting yourself down here, as the drinks are at okay prices and the food is fantastic – loads of very big burgers and salads all served at dirt cheap prices. It's chilled out, friendly and reasonable – for God's sake don't tell anyone it's here. Shit.
Mon, Wed-Sat 11am-2am, Tue 11-11, Sun 12pm-10.30pm
Meal for two: £25 (Grilled tuna steak)

■■■ Casa
375-385 Glossop Road (0114) 275 5665

Formerly the popular Hanrahans, though obviously not popular enough to hang onto its business. Still, the Casa crew have set up their repetitive bar roadshow in a pretty impressive building, but have turned it into the sort of boring and bland drinking den for which they have become nationally renowned. Specialising more as a restaurant, the food isn't spectacular but the portions are pretty big. It pretends to be quite a posh place, but fortunately that will all be rubbished when the marauding students from up the road pack it out trying to make one bottle of Metz last all night.
Food Mon-Sat 11am-10pm, Sun 12-9.30pm
Meal for two: £21 (Casa club sandwich)

■■■ The Deep End
Hillsborough (0114) 285 4000

This venue offers you just about everything you could want; cheap drinks, a massive variety of music, and even the chance to break into showbiz if you're a talented young muso. Three bars are spread between five rooms, which comes in handy if you want to ditch your boring housemate, or you just fancy a quick snog without getting prodded by your oh-so-juvenile mates. This place also has the bonus of always having some kind of entertainment, with nights such as 'Naked', 'Soul' and 'Sin'. It's good for Hillsborough that the Deep End lives here, but it would be even better for the rest of us if they moved to the city centre, so everyone could dip their toes in.
Mon-Sat 12pm-11pm, Sun 12pm-10.30pm
Meal for two: £18 (Roast dinner)

■■■ Empire Bar
25-33 Charter Square (0114) 275 2020

The Empire Bar attempts to cater for everyone's needs – the exotic and wide-ranging jugs of cocktails attract lots of young ladies,

who in turn attract lots of young men, who due to their ability to drink large quantities of alcohol boost the bar profits no end. Also a very popular venue for hen nights and work outings. Worth a visit if only to see (or enjoy – I don't know what you're into) 50-year-old local ladies trying to get in some naïve young student's boxer shorts.

Food served: Mon-Sat 11am-7pm
Meal for two: £17 (Cheeseburger)

■ ■ ■ Forum Café

Devonshire Street (0114) 272 0569

Overlooking Devonshire Green, this well-established café bar still remains one of Sheffield's most popular haunts. Since being granted a 1am extended license last year, you're likely to get a number of over excited students attempting to stumble past the bouncers after regular closing times, but it's mainly full of young couples and the odd Rastafarian enjoying the reggae. In the daytime they have a wide selection of sandwiches and snacks available. In the evenings you can get your groove on to the diverse mix of jazz, funk and hip-hop. It can get a bit overcrowded at times so it's probably not the best place to discuss wills with your grandmother, but as a cheap and trendy place to hang out with your mates, it's the perfect stop.

Mon-Sat 10am-1am, Sun 11am-5pm
Food: Salmon fillet £5.50

the forum cafe bar.
djs and live music
drinks promotions, all day every day
extensive menu
monday - saturday. 10.00 - 01.00
sunday. 11.00 - 17.00
free entry
devonshire street. sheffield. 0114 2720569
www.forum.f9.co.uk

▪▪▫ Ha! Ha!

**St. Paul's Chambers, 8-10 St. Paul's Parade
(0118) 932 3205**

Any bar that sells gentlemen's relish is alright in my book, and this brand new bar and canteen is already turning heads and rumbling stomachs. Luckily, if you too get hooked on their rather yummy brand of cooking you can also buy some of their jams and relishes to take away. Added to that it's a damn fine place to have a few jars, at night it becomes a lively melting pot of a bar that attracts the city's young upwardly mobile types. A good laugh indeed.

▪▪▪ The Halcyon Bar

113 Devonshire Street (0114) 276 6002

One of the first and still one of the best bars in town with its unique, understated brand of cool. With a gorgeously decadent and chilled-out vibe, and genuinely friendly and hospitable staff, it's a cracking place to prepare for a massive night out, or to relax and wind down from a heavy one. Guest DJs throughout the week play an eclectic mix of hip-hop, funk, jazz and house, whilst you can lounge about on plush sofas and neck large and lethal glasses of wine for £1.50. Needless to say, once in the Halcyon, the tendency is to stay for the duration.

Mon-Sat 11am-1am
Meal for two: £17 (Panninis)

halcyon bar.

sheffield's premier late bar
open. monday - saturday. 11.00 - 01.00
free entry
devonshire street
available for party hire
contact. 0114 2766002
www.thehalcyonbar.co.uk

■ ■ ■ Henry's
28 Cambridge Street (0114) 275 2342

If you ever fancy getting lost amongst some marble pillars, lush potted greenery and stone statues, then this posh cocktail bar is for you. The floors are so shiny that you can check out your profile in them, which is useful given the arse-crackingly boring clientele that this place attracts in the evening. It pretends to be posher than it really is in an effort to attract Sheffield's high society. Which actually leads to a conversation not too dissimilar to, "Have you been to that bar near Casbah with shiny floors, the one that is really up itself?", to which the response is often "Yeah. Shit innit".

Mon-Sat 8am-11pm. Food Mon-Thu 8am-9.30pm, Fri/Sat 8am-8pm
Meal for two: £21 (Meatballs & pasta)

■ ■ ■ Lloyds No.1
2 Division Street (0114) 276 5076

Not content with their ever-expanding pub empire, Wetherspoons have decided to branch out into the bar industry. Fortunately for us, they have dirt-cheap food and "beer as rain water" drinks prices, and have even decided to bless us with some music for a

change (steady on boys). Don't go turning up at the weekend in your grubby Adidas Gazelles though as it's likely that a bouncer with an insecurity problem will tell you to sod off. Personally I don't like having to dress up so that establishments, such as this, can pretend they've got an executive clientele. The former HQ for the National Union of Miners, and if Arthur knew what it was like now, he'd be round with his shovel to have a word.

Mon-Sat 10am-11pm Sun 12pm-10.30pm
Meal for two: £18 (Chicken wraps)

■■■ Lounge
Glossop Road (0114) 275 0880

Really cool café bar, it's astonishing how it can make any money as my front room is bigger than this place. Unsurprisingly the décor is minimalist chic as I guess you don't get much choice when the bar area is smaller than Jordan's underwear drawer. Nonetheless it's three or so tables do provide a chilled out and friendly atmosphere where you can spend all day having a natter. The food is pretty good too and hopefully they'll be granted an extended license so you can doss about 'til the small hours – although it's usually one in, one out from lunchtime onwards.

Mon-Thu 10am-11pm, Fri/Sat 10am-12am,
Sun 12pm-10.30pm, Food Mon-Sun 12-8
Food: (Chicken sandwich £4.25)

■■■ Mojo's
Paternoster Row (0114) 220 3605

Despite the rocky fortune of the adjoining National Centre for Popular Music, Mojo's has faired rather better. Epitomising chilled out style, throughout the week it's the perfect host for live bands as it's small enough to create the atmosphere of an intimate gig, whatever the size of the audience. At the weekend Mojo's is fast becoming the place to shake your jelly, and their club nights (including NY Sushi on Saturdays) have even managed to entice away some Leadmill devotees. Set away from the city bars this is definitely somewhere to chill out, with the added bonus that you're actually sitting in a museum – now doesn't that make you feel cultured?

Mon-Thu 7pm-12am, Fri 10.30pm-2.30am,
Sat 10.30pm-2.30am, Sun 4.30am-12pm

■■■ Revolution
1 Mappin Street (0114) 279 9250

If these bars had been around in the 1920s I reckon the cause of revolutionary communism would have been a lot more popular in

the West. Very cool and spacious vodka bar, and their list of Russian wobble juices is longer than a Docker's tea break. They have a huge list of vodkas from exotic shooters to mint choc chip – now surely historians would have been kinder to Stalin if he'd

pushed these more. The place is always rammed, and with DJs spinning tunes in the evening the has an atmosphere that's hotter than a Molotov cocktail. It's one of the best looking bars in Sheffield, and if by any chance you overdo it on their 80% yellow voddy then you can always sleep it off in one of their many plush sofas. Great food too.
Mon-Sat 12pm-11pm, Sun 12pm-10.30pm
Meal for two £20 (Sausage and mash)

■ ■ ■ RSVP
2-6 Cambridge Street (0114) 275 5152
During the week, this wanky bar is ideal to enjoy a cappuccino and chat about Pingu with your mates, but as soon as the weekend arrives it soon fills up with idiots in

Tommy Hilfiger shirts and girls in ridiculously coloured boob tubes called Stacey. If you are called Stacey and do own a boob tube then get yourself down here and have a cracking night. If you're not, limit your visits to daytimes and Sundays (on which you can often be treated to their funky resident jazz band) and chat about Pingu all you want.
Mon-Sat 11am-11pm, Sun 12pm-10.30pm
Meal for two: £16 (Cheese burger)

■ ■ ■ The Showroom
7 Paternoster Row (0114) 249 5479
A bar attached to the excellently alternative Showroom Cinema, this place is worth checking out. Not only populated by film buffs, they put on a load of groovy pre-club

top 5 for...

Late Drinks

1. The Halcyon
2. The Forum Café
3. The Showroom Café Bar
4. Brown Street
5. Brannigan's

events during the week, and late night events and record label promotions at the weekend. It has a very chilled, bohemian atmosphere that is near impossible not to warm to (especially given its lunchtime and evening menus which boast an ample array of delicious dishes). True, a lot of people in here are very aware of the cool cinema, which is actually a good thing, as it means that this is one of the few bars where it's okay to say that you liked the film more than the book – for instance Joseph Conrad's *Heart of Darkness* isn't a patch on *Apocalypse Now* – but having a drink in here beats both of them.

Mon-Thu 11am-11pm, Fri 11am-11pm,
Sun 12pm- 10.30pm
Meal for two: £28 (Pan fried duck)

■ ■ ■ Sola

North Church Street (0114) 272 9250

Tucked behind the Cathedral, this stylish underground bar is probably the coolest joint in the city. It resembles the sort of drinking dens which you tend to get in more cosmopolitan and metropolitan cities than Sheffield (is that possible?), and as such is very popular with a trendy crowd. There's also a very accomplished restaurant which serves delicious exotic food at reasonable prices. The only gripe about this place is that there's no extended license, which would make it perfect (especially as it's difficult enough to get a late drink in Sheffield). Sola is still quite new and a lot of people don't know about it, as the owners seem to be relying on word of mouth to promote the place. Well we all know that any old rabble read itchy – so that's their reputation for an exclusive clientele shafted when you lot all turn up. Ah the power of the printing press.

Mon-Sat 11-11. Closed Sun
Food Mon-Sat 12pm-9pm
Meal for two: £25 (Marinated green chicken)

pubs

www.itchysheffield.co.uk

■ ■ ■ Bankers Draft
1-3 Market Place (0114) 275 6609

This enormous pub has the cheapest prices in town and is clearly, therefore, the place to spend your life. There's a clutch of people who, perhaps, take this too literally, ending up drunk by lunchtime and trapping you in a corner to talk about Van Morrison's early hits. Aside from these few oddballs, the place is full of friendly people enjoying the average food and imported ales. It's still a Wetherspoons though, and therefore in allegiance with the devil.

Food Mon-Sat 11am-10pm,
Sun 12pm-9.30pm

■ ■ ■ The Banner Cross
971 Ecclesall Road (0114) 266 1479

Sitting atop a very steep hill makes this a fine pub to stop off for a quick one after a long walk to pick up a loaf of Hovis, but aside from that it's a pain in the ass to get to. The downstairs bar is occupied by local old duffers who evidently nipped to the bakers in 1972, and have been here ever since. The upstairs is held by the resident student populace, whose unstinting interest in the pool tables or playing Millionaire on the quiz machines makes you despair at this country's soft standards of higher education.

Food Mon-Sun 12pm-3pm

■ ■ ■ The Broadfield
452 Abbeydale Road (0114) 255 0200

There are few reasons to venture down Abbeydale Road, but this fine pub is certainly one of them. It's split into two very different sides. One side resembles the interior of a quaint village pub with its guest ales and dimly lit interior, ideal for those lazy Sunday afternoons putting the world to rights with your friends or watching the football. Alternatively, on the other side, the atmosphere is a lot livelier with a jukebox full of indie classics, great for more raucous behaviour. At last somewhere that father and son can enjoy a drink together in the same pub, although probably not in the same bar.
Food Mon-Fri 12pm-3pm and 5pm-7pm, Sat 12pm-5pm, Sun 12pm-3pm

■ ■ ■ Broomhill Tavern
484 Glossop Road (0114) 266 3470

A very small pub that's popular with the many Broomhill residents. It's very cosy, which is kind of inevitable given that it's smaller than the Rotherham F.C. executive box. A bustling student haunt, with friendly bar staff who always seem to be smiling –

although that might just be 'cos I look stupid, let me know if they're always cheerful.
Food Mon-Fri 12pm-2pm, Sat/Sun 12pm-3pm

■ ■ ■ The Cavendish
218-220 West Street (0114) 252 5781

As part of the 'It's a Scream' chain this pub is extremely student orientated with its cheap drink offers and giant Connect 4 and Jenga games. However, not everyone is a student, and for some the overriding tax dodger atmosphere may just be a little too much to take. And remember, those cheap drink offers are for yellow card-carrying students only. Shame really, as the pub is a decent size with a good jukebox and plenty of pool tables. Also their mixed grills are a fantastic unbridled celebration of carnivorous blood lust – and all the better for it.
Food Mon-Sun 12pm-6pm

■ ■ ■ Dog & Partridge
55 Trippett Lane (0114) 249 0888

A traditional pub, but it does have its peculiarities. There you sit, sipping your pint, mellowing out to the Irish tunes that are your merry accompaniment, but you're in a room that's dedicated to those great American legends, The Kennedy's. A strange concoction, but not a bad one. The staff are friendly, and will knock you up a sarnie at any point in the night, which also makes the strange surroundings that bit more accommodating. There's a hint of Sheffield in here as well, with the names of stonemasons carved into the walls. Its traditional allegiance also

shines through with a selection of guest beers and healthy looking pints, which please the city's professionals who tend to pack out this place during the week.
Food Mon-Sat 11.30am-2.30pm

■ ■ ■ The Dove and Rainbow
Hartshead Square (0114) 272 1594
The leopard print may be more common to Jackie Collins' homestead, and the purple walls to your teen angst bedroom, but this is definitely a place with its own character – an all round decent boozer. A real eclectic music policy – the jukebox and regular DJs play anything and everything from Trip Hop to Metal, so check listings for what's on, in case you accidentally stumble upon a Dolly Parton Tribute Night. Interesting wall mural too, although it could induce intense confusion and paranoia if you're on acid… but then again most things will do that when you're on acid.
Food Mon-Thu 12pm-3pm, Fri 12pm-5pm, Sat 12pm-3pm

■ ■ ■ Eighties Music Bar
128 West Street (0114) 253 6510
I could very well sit on my high horse and laugh in disgust at the thousands of people who enjoy dressing up like members of the Village People or Boney M and then 'get on down' in a John Travolta-esque manner to the 'Sounds of the 70s' CD, available from every garage forecourt for £4.99. But I too once made that mistake, I too found glittery eye shadow quirky and fun, and more times than I care to remember I have sustained an

ankle injury from jigging to disco in platform footwear. We all go through it, so do it with like-minded folk at this garishly painted fun pub which taste forgot. Of course it's a cheesy tacky boozer, but you knew that before you came in, and if you don't like it – leave.
Food Mon-Fri 12pm-3pm

■ ■ Fagans
69 Broad Lane (0114) 272 8430
This place is one of the original Irish watering holes that is actually the real McCoy, unlike the many mock Mick pubs that fill most cities. Long before every city in the country was infested by cruddy theme pubs, Fagan's was doing the Irish thing. Not the most elaborate of places, but to be honest you won't really care. It serves beer and the black stuff and lets people be themselves. It's known to have live folk groups on hand to entertain, so why not grab a pal, a pew and a pint and join in the foot tapping and thigh slapping.
Food Mon-Sat 12pm-8pm

pubspubspubspubspubspubspubspubspubspubspubspubspubspubspubspubs **pubs** ◻ ■ ■

■ ■ ■ Fat Cat
23 Alma Street (0114) 249 4801

Similar to your front room, both in size and welcoming atmosphere. A permanent fixture in the CAMRA good pub guide thanks to its wide selection of real ales. Around ten hand pulled beers available at any one time, including their home-brewed Kelham Island Bitter, plus a number of award winning ales from North Yorkshire. In addition there are continental and British bottled beers, a Belgian draught beer, fruit gin, country wines and ciders. If that's not enough there's also incredibly cheap and enjoyable bar food. An excellent pub for a relaxing Sunday lunch, just so long as you can get a seat.
Food Mon-Sun 12pm-2.30pm, Mon-Fri 6pm-7.30pm

■ ■ ■ Frog and Parrot
Division Street (0114) 272 1280

This place hides behind the façade of your average pub designed for your average drinker. However, take heed – it's far from that. The nasty conspiratorial-type people who have been put in charge have sadistically concocted their own brand of not-very-average-at-all real ale. Cunningly named 'Roger and Out', it may seem like a right laugh at the time, and if you are about to embark on a booze-fuelled jaunt around Sheffield, then a glass of this baby will probably seem rather attractive. But this is a warning: one will lead to two, two will lead to three… before you know it, you'll be psychedelic yodelling down Division Street. This is an absolutely fantastic pub in every

respect, but go easy on the 'Roger and Out'-it's 12% for God's sake, and that my friend is proper gear.
Food Mon-Sat 12pm-4pm

■ ■ ■ The Howard
57 Howard Street (0114) 278 0183

One word comes to mind to describe this pub – alright. It's traditional in style and although it's not very big there's a surprising number of seats, a pool table and fruit machines. Hallam students are a regular fixture, thanks in part to the 99p breakfasts. At the weekend expect to be drowned out by the football fans who make this place a regular stop off on their way from the station to the match.
Food 11am-2.30pm

■ ■ ■ The Hogshead
Orchard Square (0114) 275 5016

Quite popular during the day with busy shoppers and lunching business folk. In the evenings it's becoming increasingly busy, obviously tempted by the fact that this

place serves beer, and the food isn't very expensive. Unremarkable in every way – but a lot of people in Yorkshire are suspicious of new and interesting ideas. You'll be relieved to hear that this place has neither.
Food Mon-Sun 12pm-6pm

■ ■ ■ The Horn Blower
12-14 Fitzwilliams Street (0114) 272 4424
A true Irish pub in every sense of the word, The Horn Blower will bring a smirk to your face – whether it be due to the chat up lines that are thrown at you (I swear she was old enough to be my grandma), the amusing sight of watching lager drinkers try to neck Guinness, or the old guy in the corner doing an Irish jig. It's found itself a prime location therefore ensuring it will never be short of custom, plus it's the kind of homely Irish pub that makes you believe the blarney. Be warned, this is the kind of place you pop in for one, but end up on a session, so don't be surprised if this is the only place you get to on your pub crawl.
Food Mon-Sat 12-2.30pm

■ ■ ■ The Lescar
303 Sharrow Vale Road (0114) 268 8051
The Lescar's always been a bit of a dive, and let's just say it wasn't always the safest of places to while away your social time in, but then that's part of the beauty of this unassuming hangout. Hosting nightly entertainment from live jazz bands, DJs and comedians – Thursday night's 'Last Laugh' comedy club is a must, plus they serve a decent pint – the Lescar is serious value for money.

Highlight of the week through the summer has to be the Yard's Sunday Social, out back in the beer-garden. Sun yourself with a pint and soak up that sweet soul music from 4 'til 8pm. It's a very safe pub now, but if you're feeling adventurous, upon entering, elbow your way through the queue at the bar and bellow at the top of your voice 'Bar keep, a pint of fizzy and make it snappy' – that should liven up your evening.
Food Mon-Fri 12-7pm, Sat/Sun 12pm-3pm

■ ■ ■ The Nursery Tavern
276 Ecclesall Road (0114) 268 8031
A favourite with students and locals, this place is always packed and by far one of the best pubs on Ecclesall Road. Though the interior is smart and traditional (a lot of dark wood and wine racks) there's no pretentious atmosphere and, due to a recent facelift, you can now escape outside to the Italian style veranda at the front. It means that they've scrapped the snooker table, and some of its original charm, which is a good or a bad thing depending on your idea of what makes a good pub. Although on the upside, the regular offers on drinks and the exten-

sive and cheap food menu means that once you arrive, you're unlikely to leave in a hurry.
Food Mon-Fri 12pm-7pm, Sat 12pm-4pm, Sun 12pm-4.30pm

◼◼◼ O'Neill's
247-249 Fulwood Road (0114) 268 8061

This small dark pub situated in Broomhill is one of a chain that attempts to attract people with the promise of Irish men with big beards and fiery ginger women. Conversely, the people it actually attracts are bearded women and ginger men who smoke, and everyone is about as Irish as Jack Charlton. This aside, however, it's an ideal venue for St. Patrick's Day, when everyone invents their own Irish heritage. During term time this place will be rammed to the rafters, which creates a buzzing atmosphere, but isn't much good if you want to escape from it all. During the day the food is pretty good, albeit a little bit pricey. Incidentally the Guinness is shocking, drink the Murphy's instead – it's a sad day when you have to say something like that.
Food Mon-Sat 12pm-6pm, Sun 12pm-3pm

◼◼◼ The Pomona
Ecclesall Road (0114) 266 5922

If you fancy a quiet and sophisticated night out then give this one a miss. But if getting wrecked on 2 for 1 cocktails and deafening your mates on the karaoke are your scene, then The Pomona will be right up your street. It's tackier than a Balearic beach bar and inevitably attracts the student masses. Quiz nights, MTV and regular weekend DJs ensure week long entertainment, but its real

attraction is the pool table – other bars on Ecclesall Road seem to have overlooked this vital student pastime. Avoid like the plague on Bank Holidays and when the footy is on though, as hot, sweaty English lager louts make that 18-30 package-holiday experience a little too authentic.
Food Mon-Sun 12pm-7pm

◼◼◼ The Porter Brook
565 Ecclesall Road (0114) 266 5765

If they're not asleep or in a lecture they're in here (and let's face it they're not likely to be in a lecture). A hell of a lot of 'em turn out for the Monday night quiz in an effort to recreate University Challenge, but you're chances of winning any beer in this very difficult and competitive contest are slightly slimmer than the likelihood of seeing Paxman pole-dancing in Po Na Na. I'm not sure which one I'd prefer. Generally speaking though it's a decent boozer with cheap and cheerful grub. At the weekends it becomes a real meat market, where the talent is grottier than Paxman's pole.
Food Mon-Thu 11am-9pm, Sat/Sun 11am-7pm

■ ■ ■ The Porter Cottage
286 Sharrow Vale Road (0114) 268 7412

In a desperate attempt to find a down side to the excellent Porter Cottage, there's sometimes not enough seats for all the bustling punters to park their rear-ends. If you don't mind standing room only on a weekend, you can't go far wrong with the Porter providing a welcome 'proper pub' alternative to Ecclesall's plethora of noisy sports bars and snooty drinking holes. A fantastic jukebox, filled with all the great CDs you never bought, a trendy and friendly crowd, nice bar staff, plus a lively yet local vibe. I say it's the best pub in Sheffield, if you disagree get yourself down there for a night, and then lie to me on the phone the next day saying that you thought it was a bit samey.

■ ■ ■ The Slug and Fiddle
261-267 Ecclesall Road (0114) 268 2216

Despite its dodgy name, and its open plan decor bearing a striking resemblance to a cow shed, it's not a bad place to catch the footy on their ample big screens which are unrolled for any occasion. DJs spin tracks at the weekend, which give it a bit of a bar atmosphere as it fills up with attractive students and young people. What separates it from being a bar is that they do a mean fry up with their all day breakfast that even comes with chips – cool, I thought they only did that in casinos.

Food Mon-Sun 12pm-8.30pm

■ ■ ■ The Surrey
Surrey Street (0114) 275 3767

To all intents and purposes, the Surrey is a pub like any other, but with one crucial difference – this waterhole serves up house music all day long, with a solid pint, decent grub, and a couple of pool tables thrown in for good measure. A must for any self-respecting clubbing casualty, when the weekend's winding up, spend your Sunday session down the Surrey and your recovery will be well catered for, without running the risk of having S Club 7 or Steps ruin your day/appetite/game of 9-ball.

Food Mon-Fri 11am-4pm, Sat 12pm-3pm

■ ■ ■ Walkabout
Corner of West Street and Carver Street (0114) 241 3400

Australian themed pub that attracts rugby-playing gob shites by the convict ship load. Mainly a sports bar. TVs hang from every surface, so there's no where to hide as the Aussies pummel us in the cricket/rugby/tennis/tiddlywinks. Loads of cheap food, and the booze ranges from the ubiquitous innuendo-laden cocktail menu, to imported beers. The décor mainly comprises of stuffed

crocodiles and strategically positioned boomerangs, so you and your mates can make your own Gladiator-style fun and whack each other over the head with them.
Food Mon-Sun 12pm-10pm

■ ■ ■ The Washington

79 Fitzwilliam Street (0114) 276 5268

Once upon a time, you couldn't open a bag of crisps in here without getting a face full of fist. Those days, happily, are gone, but it's not so much fun now. Worth a visit to check out the Elvis clock or the immense selection of CDs behind the bar. If that wasn't enough it's also part owned by Pulp's drummer Nick Banks, and is supposedly where the band first met – sorry we mention this every year, but I still get excited about it. Good beer, good music, and a random celebrity story – what more could you ask for from a boozer?
Food Mon-Fri 12pm-2pm

■ ■ ■ West End Hotel

Glossop Road (0114) 272 5871

Its close proximity to the English Literature Department of Sheffield University means that this place is rammed at lunchtimes with students discussing how George Orwell's *1984* is a classic 20th Century text, but would have been miles better if there were kop off shower scenes and evictions like in the prop-

er telly version. It does a fine line in pub grub, which are very filling and dead cheap. It's not an amazing pub, but it's very pleasant and is the sort of place you can go to relax and have a chat in peace – which is exactly what you want from a local boozer.
Food Mon-Sun 12pm-5pm

■ ■ ■ Wetherspoons

Cambridge Street (0114) 263 9300

Cheap drinks, but no music and little atmosphere, if you like Wetherspoons you'll probably like it here. If you don't then you won't. A bit like Marmite or sodomy – you either love it or hate it.

■ ■ ■ Yorkshire Grey

69 Charles Street (0114) 275 6675

Pool tables, table football, game machines, a big screen and a beer garden. This just might be the ideal pub, lacking absolutely nothing. The large beer garden makes it a favourite in the summer as students and townies alike relax on the grass as the traffic roars past in front of them. Perfect for a pre-club, restaurant or theatre drink, seeing as it's situated slap bang in the middle of everything.
Food Mon-Sat 11.30am-7pm, Sat 12-7pm

clubs

www.itchysheffield.co.uk

■■■ The Arches
9-11 Walker Street (0114) 272 2900

Used to be known as The Arches, then it was The Underground, but everyone called it The Arches and now it's called The Arches and everyone calls it The Arches. Clear? Whatever the name not much has changed. Banging hard house, techno and trance which leads to all sorts of messy madness. This is a welcomingly attitude free club, which is just as well really given all the weirdos getting their shake on in here. Saturday night's Glasshouse offers up a spangled all nighter of uplifting house, that will keep you going until your brain resembles monkey drool. It's not nice, but it's true.

■■■ Area 51
Classified

The Sheffield clubbing scene is nationally renowned for its innovative and exciting dance venues, which is why it's no accident that you probably haven't heard of this place. Whenever the eyes of the world are focused on the steel city, this hook nosed ugly little sister is quickly hidden under the staircase, and the only way you know she's there at all is from the long trails of pissed up gurning morons. There are some fantastic clubs in Sheffield, and this place isn't one of them. In the States, the civilian public

Finger tips

RIZLA+ **It's what you make of it.**

www.rizla.com

aren't supposed to know the location of Area 51, due to the danger that it might threaten individual and national security – I feel that same sense of responsibility to you.

■ ■ ■ Bed
33-49 London Road (0114) 276 8080

Gorgeously glamorous super cool club, which has strengthened Sheffield's claim to having the strongest clubbing scene in the north. Ministry magazine love it, Danny Rampling can't stay away, and itchy reckon it's a bit of alright too. Everyone who's any-one on the DJ scene has played here knock-ing out some of the best trance, techno and hard house on the planet. The club has two floors of mayhem, plus a VIP room filled with

the type of 'Important' people that work in wanky clothes shops. With its fine wooden walls and leather seating, the place looks fantastic and attracts some of the best-dressed folk in Sheffield. Very popular with DJ celebrities whether they're working or playing – Lisa Lashes is here so often she's becoming part of the furniture and even chubby Seb Fontaine keeps coming back to get his bald patch checked. Put on your glad

rags and ask that gorgeous girl you've been after for months if she'll go to Bed with you – my money says she will.

■ ■ ■ Brown St
Brown Street (0114) 279 6959

After Kingdom, any new addition to Sheffield's clubbing scene should be treated with extreme caution. Fortunately, Brown St seem to have opted for classy rather than trashy – a sanctuary for all clubbers who have been trying to escape the hordes of drunken students and Gatecrasher-esque ravers. The whole place has a kind of futuris-tic feel but the staff are keen to make you feel at home and lardy you up with free chocolates and sweets. Friday nights are Quality, a night of the finest R'n'B, US house and garage that is less gangster (apart from the odd rude boy in the corner) and more glamour – a favourite with Sheffield's few sexy ladies. Quality indeed. Saturday's Pure offers a chilled house night that although struggling to compete with Bed, at least you have the chance of getting a drink before closing that doesn't cost you a week's wages. With loads of big names confirmed for the ensuing months, it looks pretty promising.

Hot tip

■ ■ ■ Casbah
1 Wellington Street (0114) 275 6077

You know, this clubbing lark isn't all Prada heels or glow sticks in the air. It is possible to have a damn good time without trying too hard, and Casbah's relaxed atmosphere is the place to do it in. A welcome break from the chromed furnishings of your usual dancehall, Casbah is home to a whole host of music nights from ska to indie to ROCK! Laid back Latin lovers can practice their moves at Salsa Sweet (every first and third Wednesday) and material girls can shimmy on down at True Blue (second and fourth Wednesdays), or if you fancy drastically rearranging your hairstyle by thrashing your head wildly about, you can try the appropriately named and totally rocking Mullet Rock on Fridays.

■ ■ ■ Club Adelphi
Vicarage Road, Attercliffe (0114) 243 1503

An often overlooked, but very significant club that has indirectly influenced all our lives. The 20th Century UK dance music scene would be unrecognisable without this place, as this was the original home of that little known disco, Gatecrasher, many, many years ago. Things have moved on a bit with a £1.5 million refurb overhauling this original Edwardian theatre, but the same manic, up for it vibe remains. Its location out in Attercliffe means that it's a bit of an arse to get to, but it's worth the pilgrimage as your 'avin' it' heritage would be incomplete without a stop off here. Predominantly it has three nights now of '21st Century dance' on

Fridays, the Insomniacz crew do a turn on Saturdays – which is absolutely awesome – and on Sundays they do an under 18's night which attracts the scallys from across the city, but is quite handy if you're trying to track down which little shit thieved your mobile phone.

■ ■ ■ Club Uropa
28 Eyre Street (0114) 272 8403

I've always enjoyed slating this place, but it's becoming increasingly difficult as over the last couple of years it's turned into quite a respectable little venue. It heavily targets the students during the week with cheap drinks promotions, cheap admission and party tunes, which despite being very cheesy, is a good laugh and an easy pull if you're not too picky. Things become much more interesting at the weekends when the Insomniacz crew take over the place, and there's few better ways of enjoying your day of rest.

■ ■ ■ Club Wow
Valley Centretainment, Broughton Lane (0114) 243 5670

Still remains one of the largest and most impressive clubs in Sheffield but fails to recreate the atmosphere of some of the smaller venues. It's not helped by being expensive and miles out of town. Though going there does give you the opportunity to eat your weight in saturated fat at Frankie & Benny's. Popular with townie rascals who save some money on the cab fare by picking up new shower fittings at the late night B&Q at the same time.

■ ■ ■ Club Xes
195 Carlisle Street (0114) 275 2469
See Gay Section for more details.

■ ■ ■ Corporation
1 Bank Street (0114) 276 0262
Ah, salvation from the tingly piano and diva-esque vocals so familiar with the house music raining down on your ears in your local dancing venue. Sheffield's only, and the UK's third largest, alternative club. Offering up a mix of rock, ska, hardcore, hip hop, big beat, punk, indie and thrash metal across two rooms. Hosts live music from some of the best bands from the alternative scene. Add to this a PlayStation bar in each room and an indoor skating room, and you've got one of the most rocking venues in town that is guaranteed to turn all comers into delinquents, if only for a night. No dress code but tattoo required.

■ ■ ■ The Fez Club
40 Charter Square (0114) 276 6082
In line for Mixmag's 'Small Club of the Year' award, the Fez is one of Sheffield's best-kept secrets. Po Na Na's laid back loft apartment opens its doors Thursday to Saturday, and

plays host to arguably the city's three best nights. Midweek ruckus is provided by tech-house bad boys Rhythmic (Thursdays), while Friday sees the weekend kicked firmly into touch by Remedy/Strictly Social's drum'n'bass baby, Definition, before house heavyweight Scuba moves into position to deploy some deep'n'dirty grooves, each and every Saturday night. Widely respected on the underground scene, Scuba boss Jamie Wilkins scours the planet to bring the select home crowd DJ line-ups to make even the most discerning house-head weak at the knees, so grab your snorkel and get in early – this is a slice of the good life not to be missed.

■ ■ ■ Josephine's
Fountain Precinct, Barkers Pool
(0114) 273 9810
Sheffield's oldest club. It's been going for over 20 years, it's the sort of club your parents would go to, as you have to dress up smartly (£9.99 Barratt's brogues, OK – £200 Prada trainers, NO). You can sit down and have a meal if you want, before dancing it off

Flick through the papers

to mainstream hits and cheesy classics. It's popular with mobile phone salesmen and insurance brokers, but still the bouncers will give you short shrift if you don't wear a shirt and tie – the fact you have to wear a shirt and tie to get in should be enough to put you off, if not try the fact that it's crap. FACT.

■ ■ ■ Kingdom
1 Burgess Street (0114) 278 8811

Right, the point of being a student is to get pissed, drink shed loads of cheap alcohol, be violently sick and then have sex with some easily pulled, equally shit-faced and probably ugly random. Every town has the perfect venue for this, and Kingdom is Sheffield's answer. Oh, and the teen dream music policy of Steps and S Club 7 adds to the finely honed school disco "ambience". Desperate? You really can't miss in here.

■ ■ ■ The Leadmill
6-7 Leadmill Road (0114) 221 2828
Ticket Info. 0845 300 4050

One of the best places in Sheffield for live music, attracting, as it has done for years, many top and up-and-coming bands.

Brilliant for anyone fed up with nu-metal and Limp Bizkit, who wants to get back to the good old Britpop days of Pulp and Suede. Its ability to cater for a wide range of tastes is never more in evidence than on a Monday night when there is one room for dance, one for indie and one for eighties. But whoever thought up the tastefully named 'Shag' night deserves a right good telling off for being so smutty. It's pretty appropriate though.

■ ■ ■ Mojo's
Paternoster Row (0114) 296 6060

Despite the National Centre for Popular Music dying quite spectacularly on its arse, Mojo's has rallied and rather than looking back to music greats from years gone by, it's trying to fashion out something to be remembered for. This enormous silver architectural monstrosity is now host to hard house night Exhilaration that has attracted big names such as Lisa Lashes, Mario Piu and Fergie. On Saturdays it's the new home of NY Sushi and if you're not already familiar with this little rascal (which I doubt), it knocks out some of the best hip hop, drum 'n' bass, nu house, disco, dub, funk and breaks. And if

RIZLA + www.rizla.com

that wasn't enough the Insomniacz crew knock out some hard house, with line ups that have included Andy Farley, the Tidy Boys and a hell of a lot of the Gatecrasher crowd. It may look like an ill formed steel teapot, but by God have they got something brewing inside.

■ ■ ■ Niche
87-91 Sidney Street (0114) 270 0996

It's midday on a Sunday and whilst the average person is contemplating a fry up, the last of the die-hard clubbers are crawling out of the black pit that is Niche, squinting at the sun and trying to remember what day it is (and possibly their name). Open 12am-12pm, this is a scary clubbing experience that would be better suited to a dingy New York basement than sunny Sheffield. What attracts the crowds of people that pack this joint to the brim every week is the music. It's the raw sound of the underground; uplifting house and pumping speed garage getting your toes twitching and your body grinding.

■ ■ ■ Orchis
24 Carver Street (0114) 273 8677

Don't be fooled by the subterranean location, Orchis is about as underground as a space station. A bit of a novelty venue – one that wears thin fast – the club has held onto its upbeat vibe, despite swapping some of its better nights for the usual townie fare of R'n'B, garage and tacky house. Sundays represent something of a departure, with New York Soul putting on a better than average party, but Orchis is long overdue a class injection.

■ ■ ■ Planet
429 Effingham Road (0114) 244 9033
See Gay Section for more info. If you want.

■ ■ ■ Po Na Na
40 Charter Square (0114) 276 6082

Done out in the same vein of interior design as Yoda's gaff on Tattoine, there's a certain something about Po Na Na – something

Hand book

that smacks of class. Since its arrival in Sheffield, this unique club has gone from strength to strength, and now plays host to some of the city's most respected nights. Tech-house/techno connoisseurs Remedy roll out the rug to welcome guest DJs from across the globe each and every Friday. Past highlights have included Stacey Pullen and Andrew Weatherall – while Saturday sees a hip-hop/breaks invasion in the form of Phonetics, bringing head-nodders the likes of Jeru the Damager (Gang Starr), and Task Force. With midweek support from Sheffield's likely lads, Strictly Social, this is one nightspot not to be sniffed at.

■ ■ ■ The Republic
112 Arundel Street (0114) 276 6777
Best known for the legendary Gatecrasher, The Republic attracts hardcore clubbers from all over the country. For the thriftier, or less flamboyantly dressed, clubber weekdays are more favourable. Blessed (Mondays), 'Crashers Little Bro' plays mainly

trance and hard house, Jigsaw (Tuesdays) hosts the vomit inducing 'drink as much as you can' dentist's chair and Disco 2001 (Thursday) plays a variety of house, R'n'B and chart classics, and is often cited as the best student night in Sheffield. The Republic can generally be relied on for a good night, although the expansive, if confusing, three floor industrial layout can make it difficult to find people, especially after a trip on that dentist's chair.

■ ■ ■ Roundhouse
Ponds Forge International Sports Centre, Sheaf Street (0114) 275 0757
Oh the irony of it all, a club directly below a gym. Laugh at the late night gym junkies leaving with their red faces and sweaty leotards, as you embark on another night of the the Silk Cut and cider diet. Cheap drinks, party tunes and those people in Afro wigs to laugh at on 70s night... only the Pope could resist.

■ ■ ■ Unit
Trafalgar Court, Milton Street (0114) 278 4540
Despite the departure of NY Sushi this is still one of the baddest boys in town. Anyone who's anyone in the DJ world has jumped aboard the decks here in the last three years. Their Saturday night extravaganza All Points North is a veritable beast of breaks and beats where you can quite often expect to catch the likes of Fabio and Grooverider, or rising stars like Paul Wolford. The sushi has gone off, but they're still cooking. Boom.

club listings

For more up-to-date reviews, previews and listings check www.itchysheffield.co.uk

All listings details are subject to change at short notice, and should therefore be used as a guide only.

Club	Night	Music	Price
MONDAY			
The Leadmill	University of Shag	Indie/Dance/Britpop	£2 b4 11 £1 NUS /£4 after
Jospehines	Soul Night	Soul	£3 b4 11pm/£4 after
Casbah	Phat City	Modern Guitar/Nu Metal	Free entry
Kingdom	Vodka Sheffield	Comm Dance, party pop	-
The Republic	Blessed	Disco, R&B, Hip Hop	£4
TUESDAY			
Bed	Layed	House, Trance	-
Casbah	Bandwesier	Live Bands	Free entry
The Republic	Jigsaw	-	£3/£2.50 N.U.S.
Leadmill	Hell	Dance Anthems & 70s	£3
Orchis	Pink	Camp Classics	£3.50
WEDNESDAY			
Casbah	Salsa Suite	Salsa	Free entry
Club Uropa	Heat	Commercial House & Garage	Free entry
Fez Club	Strictly Social	Dub, Breaks and Beats	-
Kingdom	Student Night	House, Trance, Garage	£3
Leadmill	Planet Earth	80s, Retro, R&B	£4
Po Na Na	Obsession	Soul, Funk, RnB and Garage	£3 b4 11pm, £4 after
THURSDAY			
Brown Street	Muesli	Bit of everything	Free entry
Bed	Souled Out	R&B, Garage, Funk, Hip Hop	£3.50/£2.50 (concessions)
Casbah	Shell Suit	Hip Hop, late 80s early 90s	Free entry
Club Uropa	Versus	DJ contest	£3
Fez Club	Stomp	Indie Classics	-
Leadmill	FAB	Pop and R&B	£4
Po Na Na	Whistle Pop	Pop & Commercial Dance	£3
The Republic	Disco 2001	Chart Anthems	£4/£3 N.U.S.

Take a leaf out of our book

FRIDAY

Arches	Headcharge	Techno, trance, big beat	£10/£8 concessions
Bed	Better Days	Club Classics, Anthems	£5/£4 concessions
Brown Street	Quality	Funk	£4 B4 11.30pm/£6 after
Casbah	Mullet Rock	Rock	£3
Club Uropa	Desire	Commercial Dance & R&B	£3
Fez Club	Remedy	-	-
Fez Club	DEF:N:T:ON	Drum & Bass, Hip Hop, Breaks	-
Kingdom	Come Together	House	-
Orchis	Tonic	Dance, Speed Garage	£4
Po Na Na	TOP	Deep Tech Tribal Grooves	£5
The Republic	Bubblegum	80s & 90s	£5/£3.50
The Roundhouse	Atomic	80s & 90s	£3.50

SATURDAY

Bed	Bed	House	£12/£10 concessions
Brown Street	Pure	Funky Vocal House	£2 members, £4/£6 after 11
Casbah	Hellraisers	Classic Indie	£3
Club Adelphi	Flirt	Commercial Dance	Free B4 11pm, £3 after
Club Uropa	Pure	Uplifting Commercial Dance	£3
Fez Club	Scuba	House	£7/£5 members
Kingdom	-	Commercial House	-
Orchis	Shugah	R&B, UK Garage	£5
Po Na Na	Phonetics	Funk, Jazz, Breaks & Beats	£5
The Republic	Gatecrasher	House	£15/£12.50 NUS
The Roundhouse	Bus Stop	70s night	£6

SUNDAY

Club Uropa	VAT	Vocal House and Trance	£5

At **www.itchysheffield.co.uk**, you'll find articles on all the best music and events, with stuff from some of the finest independent magazines in the UK, including...

   Chaser

Big Daddy: Hip hop, beats and culture

Deuce: The UK Garage Bible

Knowledge: Drum 'n' bass and breakbeat

Straight no Chaser: Jazz and all things funky

Playlouder.com: Like NME but different

www.itchysheffield.co.uk

RIZLA + www.rizla.com

gay

www.itchysheffield.co.uk

In the words of an old Yorkshire duffer "The whole world's queer, save me and thee, and even thee's a bit queer". Although Sheffield isn't exactly renowned for it's gay scene, it's array of pulsating clubs and heaps of young party people, means the place is starting to hold its own and offering a big night out for pink punters. After all, in a city that's renowned for The Full Monty, hard man Prince Naseem, and some whacking great steel rods – who could resist?

■■ Clubs

■■ Climax @ Sheffield Uni S.U.
Western Bank (0114) 2228673

Yorkshire's biggest gay night, and has to be the most fun you can have in a public place. Lively, tacky and unashamedly pop, it's a real bummer that it's only on once a month. Hordes of bright young things mingle with slightly bemused older things. It has one of the best dykes-to-fags ratio around.
£3 adv/£4 on the door. 2nd Fri of the month in term time, 10pm-2am

■■ Club Xes
195 Carlisle Street (0114) 275 2469

Formerly the Norfolk Arms, it's still a bit like a traditional pub with pool tables and bar snacks available. This friendly, gay-orientated club spins those 80s disco classics you once owned but regrettably threw out in your teenage angst years. There's also the chance to raid your mum's wardrobe for TV night, or grab that lumberjack shirt and leather trousers for the legendary bears evening that attracts biker fags from far and wide.
Sat 8pm-12am, Sun 8pm-10.30pm

Luxury Voodoo @ The Unit
Milton Street (0114) 2580470

A once-a-month radical night with the music happily being a mix of everything you can envisage that isn't Kylie or Madonna. The venue is modern industrial with Mediterranean leanings and the crowd veers between pretentious arty types and off-their-face students, but happily no style-obsessed queens.
2nd Wed of the month, 10pm-2am

Planet
429 Effingham Road (0114) 261 7510

Sheffield's only full-time gay club, and with limited full-time competition it's still pretty damn good. The sexy DJs spin dance classics and cheesy club anthems that attract Sheffield's gay girls and boys. It's not too pricey to get in, especially if you grab some of the flyers that are on offer at Bar-Celona or The Cossack beforehand.
Thu-Sat 9pm-2am, Sun 9pm-12am

Bars

Bar-Celona
387 Attercliffe Road (0114) 244 1492

Subtly Spanish-themed pub which gets live- ly at the weekends when it's usually the last stop on the way to the club. Loud music, a DJ in drag and the occasional stripper make it very much a gay man's venue, although the gay girls have a blast too. Drinks are well priced, and it has all the gay papers; stop off here on your way to Planet to get a flyer for discounted entry.
Fri-Sat, 8.30-11pm Sun, 8.30-10.30pm

Pubs

The Cossack
45 Howard Street (0114) 263 4921

A hugely popular old-styled pub for a mixed gay crowd. Monday is quiz night, Tuesday 80's dance music, Wednesday buffet night, Thursday karaoke, Friday and Saturday are dance music nights, and on Sunday they also do a fine line in good value pub lunches. So you can happily spend every night in The Cossack.
Mon-Sat 12pm-11pm, Sun 12pm-10.30pm

Club Lukas
195 Carlisle Street (0114) 2752469

Despite calling itself a club, it's really just a pub with a late license. During the week it's pretty quiet, but as the weekend approaches it picks up, particularly when it plays host to the monthly bears night and the twice-monthly tranny nights which pack the place to the rafters. Décor is Euro-techno mixed with traditional pub, and it's very much a man's bar. The bar staff are friendly, drinks are cheap, and the liquor flows late into the night throughout the week, which means that most people stay for the whole hog.
Mon-Thu, 9pm-1am Fri-Sat, 8-12pm Sun, 8-10.30pm

shopping

www.itchysheffield.co.uk

■■ Shopping Centres/Area

■■ Crystal Peaks
Crystal Peaks (0114) 251 0457

Although it sounds like it's named after some fairy at the bottom of the garden, this faded shopping complex is far from a magical delight. I know that shopping centres are hardly epitomes of class and style, but when compared to Sheffield's legendary Meadowhall, this once magnificent shopping mecca does look a little ropey now. Stuck up in the hills, you'll have to make a special journey to check out its wares, but why bother when you'll probably bump into those drop outs who bullied you at school who now stack shelves and arrange coat hangers for a living... actually, go and laugh at the gits, they never did you any favours.

■■ Ecclesall Road

Often referred to as the Golden Mile of Sheffield shopping, Ecclesall Road provides a break from the hustle and bustle of the town centre. By far the most cosmopolitan area of the city, it offers a mixture of specialist shops covering gifts, clothes, music, home ware, jewellery and plants, and is bound to cater for whatever it is you desire. Café bars, restaurants and a great number of pubs provide a well-needed break for your aching feet during the day and as the sun goes down it fills up with both locals and students for the best party atmosphere around.

■■ The Forum
127-129 Devonshire Street
(0114) 272 0569

The Devonshire Quarter has long been regarded as the coolest place to shop and

hang out in Sheffield, and The Forum was the catalyst for the development of this area. Now in its 8th year, The Forum shopping centre still offers some of the most diverse boutiques around, attracting Sheffield's beautiful people by the bucket load. Voted one of the UK's top shopping centres by Cosmopolitan magazine – and they do a hell of a lot of shopping. With groovy offerings from Frox, Elevator, Garage, Bliss, Freshmans and Yes Orange, you can find a fab array of cool clothing. There's also jewellery, lava lamps and the like in Fuse, plus a haven for fans of bongs and pipes at Golden Harvest. There's also some top tunes from Freebass Records. Plans to convert the upstairs floor to a pool hall are underway, but as yet no concrete changes have been made.
Mon-Sat 9am-6pm

▪ ▪ ▪ Meadowhall
1 The Oasis 0845 757 3618
Regarded as a national treasure by retail therapists, this huge shopping centre is now synonymous with Sheffield. As one of the biggest shopping centres in the country it's no surprise that virtually every high street brand you can think of puts in an appearance somewhere, plus three supermarkets and a selection of alternative shops found in 'The Lanes'. Added to that there's an extensive food hall and an 11 screen cinema. If you don't fancy driving, there's an efficient train and tram service to whizz you there and back. Also, if you feel that your life is lacking excitement then pay this place a visit on Christmas Eve or the first day of the January sales, and battle it out with some of the most aggressive and manic shoppers you've ever seen.
Mon-Fri 10am-9pm, Sat 9am-7pm, Sun 11am-5pm

▪ ▪ ▪ Orchard Square
41 Orchard Square (0114) 275 9992
This pocket size city centre shopping courtyard is kitted out with a Waterstone's, some chain pubs and some craft shops – presumably for Sheffield's bevy of knitting folk to stock up on their wool. I don't really want to mention the Swiss Alps style chiming clock, but for any tourists reading this it may be the best piece of Sheffield architecture you'll see.

▪ ▪ ▪ Women's Fashion

▪ ▪ ▪ Bliss
**The Forum, Devonshire Street
(0114) 276 3565**
You, Lipsy, Balis & Knight, Ange and Amazing.
Mon-Sat 10am-6pm

▪ ▪ ▪ Etam
**79 High Street, Meadowhall
(0114) 256 9731**
Mon-Fri 10am-9pm, Sat 11am-7pm, Sun 11am-5pm

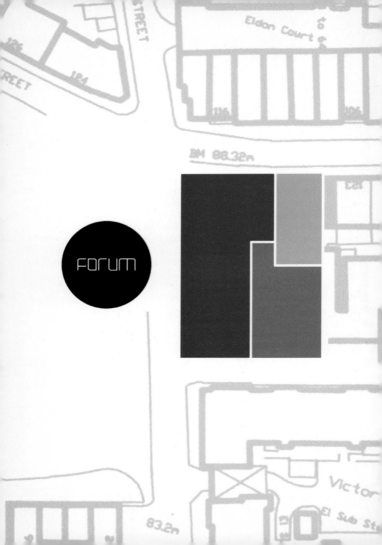

forum

the forum shops.

"one of britain's top shopping centres"
cosmopolitan magazine

everything you need all under one roof.
dressed up. dressed down. street. casual. vintage.
music. gifts. bongs. body piercing. jewellery. footwear.
bags. hats. candles. watches. etc.etc.

monday - saturday. 10.00 - 18.00
devonshire street. sheffield. 0114 2720569
www.forum.f9.co.uk

■ ■ ■ Frox
The Forum, Devonshire Street
(0114) 276 0770
Transit, Ghost, Whistle, Jimmy Jules, French
Connection and Alexander Campbell.
Mon-Sat 10am-6pm

■ ■ ■ Karen Millen
30 Park Lane, Meadowhall
(0114) 256 8920
Mon-Fri 10am-9pm, Sat 9am-7pm,
Sun 11am-5pm

■ ■ ■ Name
100 Devonshire Street (0114) 270 0043
Set in the stylish end of town, Name's collection of women's clothing is full of designer
names (hence the 'Name'). Well tailored
clothes and individual pieces make this
shop well worth a visit, though it isn't cheap.
An added bonus though is that they offer a
free alterations service (the clothes, not
you), which is very handy for all those freak-
ishly proportioned people out there.
Mon-Sat 10am-5.30pm

■ ■ ■ Oasis
16 Park Lane, Meadowhall (0114) 256 8652
Mon-Fri 10am-9pm, Sat 9am-7pm,
Sun 11am-5pm

■ ■ ■ Versa Woman
108 Devonshire Street (0114) 279 6145
Miss Sixty and Boxfresh.
Mon-Sat 10am-6pm

■ ■ ■ Yes Orange
The Forum, Devonshire Street
(0114) 273 9511
A regular fixture in The Forum now for over
seven years, this place is the only UK stockist
of Yes Orange. They specialise in ladies casual
and evening wear. The majority of the
designers are Sheffield based which ensures
that there's plenty of feedback and that
orders and commissions can be dealt
with quickly.
Mon-Sat 10am-6pm

■ ■ ■ Men's Fashion

■ ■ ■ Brother 2 Brother
112 Devonshire Street (0114) 273 7546
In a city renowned for its tight-fistedness,
Brother 2 Brother is something of an anom-
aly. It's a mystery where its clientele appear
from, but evidently there are plenty of dapper chaps in Sheffield who think nothing of
forking out 500 quid for a cashmere cardi-
gan. Labels include Vivienne Westwood,
Dries Van Noten and Alexander McQueen –
if you don't have a gold card when you
come in here, you can certainly forget about
ever getting one by the time you leave.
Flash togs though.
Mon-Sat 10am-6pm

■ ■ ■ Burton Menswear
29 The Moor (0114) 272 5385
Mon-Wed 9.30am-5.30pm, Thu 9.30am-
7pm, Fri/Sat 9.30am-6pm, Sun 11am-5pm

■ ■ Envy
20 High Street, Meadowhall
(0114) 256 8647
Mon-Fri 10am-9pm, Sat 9am-7pm,
Sun 11am-5pm

■ ■ Eton
38 Division Street (0114) 270 0829

Loads and loads of lads labels including Replay, Dolce & Gabanna, Diesel, Ted Baker, Boxfresh, French Connection and Paul Smith, plus a few new offerings from Dynasty, Armed Response, Urban Paranoia, and Japanese dapper designers Etienne Ozeki. The prices can be a bit steep, but the clobber is gorgeous.
Mon-Sat 9.30am-5.30pm

■ ■ Limeys
22-24 Chapel Walk (0114) 279 8444
More upmarket than Rockport, but still about as original as Corn Flakes, Limeys provide essential tailoring for all those desperate to impress at Bed this Saturday night. Large offerings from Hugo Boss, Paul Smith, Armani, Nicole Farhi, Stone Island, DKNY, Ted Baker and Henri Lloyd.
Mon-Fri 9.30am-6pm, Sat 9am-6pm

■ ■ Name
36 Division Street (0114) 275 773
Slightly more down-to-earth prices than some of its Division Street counterparts, and a fine selection of understated tailoring makes parting company with your cash a slightly more pleasant experience.
Mon-Sat 10am-5.30pm

■ ■ Unisex

■ ■ Alley
25 Chapel Walk (0114) 273 1467
One of the best places to get yourself suited and booted, if you want to keep up with the in crowd (without having to rob your granny), then Alley should be right up your street, if you'll pardon the pun.
Mon-Sat 10am-6pm

■ ■ Ark
114 Devonshire Street (0114) 272 2561
OK'ish skate and slacker style casual clothes that are pretty funky and reasonably priced, but far from original. Pretty good clobber if you want to dress like you're more interesting and original than you really are – the only problem is that you're likely to be rumbled by the 8000 or so students all wearing the same outfit.
Mon-Sat 10am-6pm

■ ■ Elevator
The Forum, Devonshire Street
(0114) 272 8826
Like a trip down the shops with Mr Benn, where will the elevator take us today? We can

! 🗋 🖉 From	Subject
✉ itchycity.co.uk	Weekend offers to your inbox

never be sure, but it's always to a place with a touch of class. You'll find displays from Sharp Eye, Vex Generation, All Saints, Dexter Wong, John Richmond, and Eye. Sheffield's most original clothes store – a penthouse among all the other basement boutiques.

Mon-Sat 10am-6pm

■ ■ ■ Mandarini
The Forum, Devonshire Street
(0114) 278 1841

Cool casual clothes store stocking independent brands including Work, Rude, and Chunk.

Mon-Sat 10am-6pm

■ ■ ■ Sumo
96 Devonshire Street (0114) 275 7143

If today's skateboarder is judged more by the weight of his wallet than by the height of his ollie, then Sumo's skaters must be the best in town. Skate gear from Etnies, Nike, Animal, Globe and Airwalk. Nice threads admittedly, but if you're still in school, you'd best get yourself a sponsor.

Mon-Sat 10am-6pm, Sun 12pm-4pm

Andy, 21, Snowboard technician

When you're not skating where do you sink some jars? Frog & Parrot
And where do you get your munch on? Ask!
Where rocks? Corporation
Where do you get your clobber? Forum
What's the best thing about Sheffield? Sheffield Ski Village
And the worst? You can't skate through town

■ ■ ■ Unlimited
8 Eldon Court/100 Division Street
(0114) 273 7827

Sporting an impressive selection of bowling shoes and darts shirts, Unlimited knocks out some not-bad threads at not-bad prices. Check out the sales for some cracking bargains, when you can kit out the whole darts team for the price of some quality arrows. The fish tank is worth a look too, apparently its sole inhabitant is the oldest goldfish in Sheffield, but with the Devonshire chippy on the other side of the street, for how long?

Mon-Sat 10am-5.30pm

top 5 for...
Eats To Impress
1. Rafters
2. The Mediterranean
3. Brasserie Leo
4. Beauchief Hotel
5. Bahn Nah

IT'S THE DREAM JOB.

■ ■ ■ Retro and Second Hand

■ ■ ■ Freshmans
Carvey Street (0114) 272 8333

If the 70s was the decade that style forgot, then a visit to Freshmans may surprise you. Carrying the largest selection of second hand clothing in Yorkshire, they hold a vast range of 70s fashions and memorabilia. The proprietor, Paul Lincoln, spends most of his time combing the East Coast of America, plus San Francisco and Miami in search of the finest vintage looks. There's a smaller branch in The Forum which does a fine line in limited edition Levis, whilst the Carvey Street store has to be seen to be believed; a bustling arrays of shirts, suits, wigs, Choppers and scooter bikes. The prices are very reasonable, which unsurprisingly makes it a firm favourite with local students, but it's also worth a visit just to relive your youth.
Mon-Sat 10am-6pm

■ ■ ■ Southern Playa
14 Furnival Gate (0114) 281 4656
Fresh outta da ghetto – all be it the best dressed hood on the south side. No rude

boy's wardrobe would be complete without a visit to Southern Playa.
Mon-Sat 9am-6pm, Sun 11am-4am

■ ■ ■ Records

■ ■ ■ Con Brio
95 Division Street (0114) 275 1880
If Buena Vista Social Club got your loins a-stirring and you fancy something with a lit-

tle bit more rhythm than S Club 7, take a trip to Con Brio where Pete, the stores owner, will quite happily steer you in the right direction for anything from Latin beats and salsa

BUT YOU DON'T WANT TO LOOK DESPERATE.

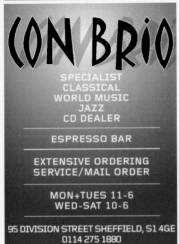

moves to jazz melodies and classical tunes. Grab a coffee, sit down on some wicker and try before you buy, in this popular little haven to good music.
Mon 11am-6pm, Tue-Sat 10am-6pm

■ ■ ■ Fopp
40 Division Street (0114) 249 1184
Located on trendy Division Street this cramped independent record store is probably one of the best you'll find. Whether it's Lou Reed, Otis Redding or Radiohead that you're looking for, this little beauty will stock them all and probably for only a fiver each. Catering for all genres of music at excellent prices, this shop is one to avoid if you're trying to save money. Although the place gets extremely busy (especially at weekends), the staff will happily take time out to recommend artists as opposed to merely grunting "Who's Iggy Pop?". Boasting a good vinyl section and a fine selection of cult videos and books, Fopp is a blessing in disguise come Christmas time, when you have to buy loads of presents. One of Sheffield's unspoilt treasures.
Mon-Sat 9.30am-6pm, Sun 11am-4.30pm

■ ■ ■ Forever Changes
533 Ecclesall Road (0114) 267 9787
The regularly changing collections of CDs and vinyl mean that frequent visits are necessary just to keep up. There's a huge stock of quality CDs which start at about £6 with vinyl starting at as little as a quid a pop. There's a large array of dance music, plus promos you never thought you'd get your mitts on. Open everyday, and with friendly and chatty staff it's well worth stopping off for a while – after all Ecclesall Road is a bloody long bit of road.
10am-7pm, 11am-5pm

■ ■ Freebass Records
The Forum, Devonshire Street
(0114) 281 2127

Drum'n'bass, trance and mainstream house are well represented, and if they're out of the latest choice cut that you're after, there's a pretty good chance that they'll be able to order it for you. You need this in your life, or something like that.

Mon-Sat 10am-6pm, Sun 11am-5pm

■ ■ HMV
High Street (0114) 275 1445

Oodles of singles and albums, DVDs, videos, computer games, books, dozens of listening posts and loads of pictures of Nipper the Dog – he influenced Snoop Doggy Dog you know? We all know what HMV is like, and unsurprisingly this place is no different.

Mon-Sat 9am-6pm, Sun 11am-4pm

■ ■ Noise Annoys
53 Howard Street (0114) 276 9177

Soft rock, hard rock, industrial rock, everything bar Brighton rock.

Mon-Fri 10am-5.30pm, Sat 10am-5pm

■ ■ Polar Bear
547 Ecclesall Road (0114) 267 1823

With a large selection of new and used CDs at very reasonable prices, it's difficult to pass by this place without going in every day. They'll pay you handsomely for your used CDs and happily have a natter to you about what tunes would best suit what you're after – even if you are looking for Gary Barlow's

the polar bear

compact discs bought, sold & exchanged

new releases ordering service available

286 ecclesall road, sheffield
tel/fax 0114 267 1823

mon - sat 10am - 6pm
sun 11am - 5pm

back catalogue. With everything from Tom Jones to Tom Watts, I'd swap my last glacier mint for an extra five minutes in here.

Mon-Sat 10am-6pm, Sun 11am-5pm

■ ■ ■ Record Collector
233-235 Fulwood Road (0114) 266 8493
Recommended by all the top music mags, Record Collector is a must for any serious music fan looking for something away from the mainstream. Helpful staff and a massive range ensure that you won't go away empty-handed.
Mon-Sat 10am-6pm

■ ■ ■ The Store
107 Devonshire Street (0114) 278 4933

The Store's head honcho Mark Jones gets out of bed, eats his breakfast and launches a daily crusade against the music world's purveyors of pap. One of the nation's finest, let alone Sheffield's, this is a record shop with few rivals when it comes to quality, and the customer-friendly pricing policy puts DJs before dollars. With some of the freshest cuts around, if it's not in the Store, chances are it ain't worth having but if it itches, scratch it – stick your 'must-haves' in Mr. Jones' orders book and they'll be with you on the flip-side. If only all record shops were made this way.
Mon-Sat 11am-6pm

■ ■ ■ Virgin Megastore
3 Orchard Square (0114) 273 1175
If you aren't familiar with Virgin's wares, then which planet have you been on? Loads of CDs, vinyl, DVDs, computer games and books (including this little beauty). If you seriously are a Virgin virgin, then check it out – it's mighty fine.
Mon-Sat 9am-6pm, Sun 11am-5pm

■ ■ ■ Books

■ ■ ■ Blackwell's
220 Fulwood Road (0114) 266 0820
156-160 West Street (0114) 273 8906
Sheffield Hallam Uni, Pond Street
(0114) 275 2152
Sheffield Uni, Mappin Street
(0114) 278 7211
This bookshop is linked to the University and has always, therefore, got a good supply of medical textbooks, mathematics formulae booklets and Jane Austen novels. Like Waterstone's, you can usually find what you're looking for, but if they haven't got that coveted roof thatching manual, then they'll happily order you one in. Although they mainly sell academic books you can still buy Posh's biog, and other brain dead trash. Not cheap, but then again, not many bookshops are these days. Although they do sell this book, and we're not dear, more's the pity.
Mon-Sat 9am-5.30pm, Sun 11am-5pm

■ ■ ■ Waterstone's
24-26 Orchard Square (0114) 272 8971
Meadowhall (0114) 256 8495
Unsurprisingly this bookshop is full of books. Big books, small books, books with glossy covers, books made from recycled

WHATEVER TURNS YOU ON *Virgin* megastores

er scientists alike. You can normally get a good deal on contemporary fiction, so it's probably worth a visit before heading off on holiday. You don't, of course, have to read the thing but it is a good alibi when you're checking out the talent on the beach.
Mon-Sat 9am-6pm, Sun 11am-5pm

■■ Miscellaneous

■■ Forbidden Planet
12 Matilda Street (0114) 276 9475
Scarily knowledgeable staff can point you in the right direction for all your cult comic, film and TV memorabilia. It's not all Star Trek either, the surging hormones of today's teenager have made all things Buffy a veritable goldmine – no doubt due to its gripping storylines and moralistic lessons yeah?
Mon-Fri 10am-5.30pm, Sat 9.30am-5.30pm

paper, books about pigeons and even books which teach you how to read a book. It's pretty much got every kind of book you're going to need for getting through life and will therefore satisfy historians and comput-

entertainment

www.itchysheffield.co.uk

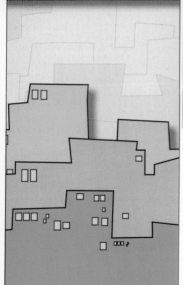

◼◼◻ Cinema

Odeon Cinema
Arundel Gate (0114) 272 3981

Everyone has one, and so does Sheff. Formerly cheap and cheerful, old as the hills cinema, but they've now had a refit and are quite dear. Boo.

Mon, Wed, Thu, Fri before 5pm £3.60 for all, after 5pm and weekends £4.70 adults, £3.60 conc. and children. Tue £2.50 for all.

◼◼◼ The Showroom Cinema
7 Paternoster Row (0114) 275 7727 (box office), (0114) 279 6006 (recorded info)

Independent cinemas are hard to come by these days, but luckily for us in Sheffield The Showroom is one of the best around. If you're not satisfied with simply watching Arnie flexing his muscles or Ben Stiller getting his family jewels trapped in fences, then head for this superb cinema. Showing a variety of British, American and foreign films, this is definitely the place for the more cultured amongst us. On Mondays and Tuesdays, students can catch any film for £2, and at other times prices are still very reasonable. The adjoining bar means that you don't have to

rush off either, leaving you free to chat about Ang Lee's special effects until midnight.
Weekdays before 5pm £3.70 adults, £2.50 under 15s/conc.
After 5pm and Sat and Sun £4.70 adults, £3.50 under 15s/conc.

■ ■ Warner Village Cinemas
**The Oasis, Meadowhall Centre
(0114) 256 9825/256 9222**

11 whole screens with the obligatory cushioned seats, surround sound, handy drink holders on the chair arms and enough sugary confectionery to make your mum go ballistic. Speaking of which, does she know you're out on a school night?
Tickets £4.50 (£3.60 NUS).

■ ■ Theatres

■ ■ The Crucible
55 Norfolk Street (0114) 249 6000
Still most famous for its annual Embassy Snooker Championship, this established venue boasts an excellent programme throughout the year. Attracting big names such as Hollywood pretty boy Joseph Fiennes, warbling wordsmith John Hegley and even comic legend Ken Dodd, The Crucible offers a varied set of acts. With popular performances you have to book early, but with more contemporary productions, you can usually get a £5 standby ticket on the day of performance.
Tickets £7.50 (matinées), £15 (evenings).

itchy sms @
www.itchysheffield.co.uk

secret gig
tomorrow 8pm @

■ ■ ■ Lyceum Theatre
55 Norfolk Street (0114) 249 6000

Closely linked to The Crucible, the Lyceum tends to host events by touring companies. A traditional arch theatre has occupied the same site for over a hundred years. It offers a diverse range of stage (whether it be drama, dance, opera, comedy or music). Both the RSC and The Royal National Theatre regularly tour here, recent productions of The Duchess of Malfi and Westside Story are among many of the recent performances to have trod the boards here.
Tickets £10- £20 (depending on the production).

■ ■ ■ Snooker/Pool

■ ■ ■ Abbey Snooker Club
Abbeydale Road (0114) 258 0414
More tables than an 11+ maths exam, a bar and food available throughout the day. It's a damn good place to get some cueing action and practice for your appearance at The Crucible next year.
Mon-Sun 10.30-11pm. Day pass £2, 12 month membership £13. 10.30am-6pm £2.50 per hour. 6pm-close £3.40 per hour

■ ■ ■ Riley's American Pool & Snooker Centre
Mansfield Road
(0114) 239 2207
It's open 24 hours, so there's plenty of time to practice if you're really crap and you can tell all your mates that you were up 'til 6am potting the pink. The bar shuts at 11pm, but you can get food at any time of the day or night. Hustle.
Open 24 hours. £7 membership. Pool £5.15 per hour, snooker £4.15 per hour.

■ ■ ■ Live Music

Pulp, Moloko and Martin Fry all developed their soft sounds amidst the very rough delights of dear old Sheff, so unsurprisingly there's one or two choice spots worth checking out for live music. The most renowned is probably **The Leadmill** – the list of bands that have played here in the last twenty years reads like a 'Who's Who' in British music. Even Menswear have played. If you fancy something a bit more hardcore then there's **Corporation**, Sheffield's only alternative club where you can catch a bit of rock, ska, hip hop, punk, big beat and indie. For less famous acts there's **The Deep End** in Hillsborough, which has live music on every night. In a similar vein there's **The Lescar** (although better known for its comedy nights), where you can catch live jazz bands in what is a pretty good boozer. Alternatively **The Bistro Casablanca** knocks out some fine jazz music and great Mediterranean food.

entertainmententertainmententertainmententertainmen **entertainment**

■■ Comedy

■■ Last Laugh @ The Lescar
Sharrow Vale Rd (0114) 268 8051

Decent stand-up comedy in Sheffield is a bit thin on the ground, but you can grab some gags at the "Last Laugh Comedy Club". Run by local comedy legend Toby Foster, the club has grown over the 90s and just about every notable comic on the circuit has played this place at some point. A particular favourite of Channel 4's Peter Kay and Johnny Vegas, who often pop up at short notice and do a turn. They also do open mic spots during the evening, so any young hopefuls can turn up, chance their arm, and die on their arse.

Check www.itchysheffield.co.uk for listings.
Advance tickets available from Forever Changes (0114) 267 9787. Shows every Thursday, doors 8.30pm.

■■ Bowling

■■ Fastlane Bowl
1 Richmond Road (0114) 269 9622
Live life in the fast lane – ha ha. Sorry, it's a bowling alley, there's a minimal amount you can write about it.
Mon-Sun 10am-12am. 10am-6pm 1 game £2.75, 6pm-close 1 game £3.60.

■■ Firth Park Bowling Centre
Sicey Avenue (0114) 242 5152
Mon-Sun 9.30am-11.30pm.
1 game Mon-Fri before 6pm £2.30.
All other times £3 per game.

■■ Hollywood Bowl
Valley Centretainment, Broughton Lane (0114) 244 4333
Mon-Sun 10am-12pm. £3.75 adults, £2.75 children (£8.90 for 3 games).

■■ Activities

■■ Avago Indoor Karting Centre
Whitelee Road, Swinton 01709 578 707
Prove your boyfriend, and his "women drivers" comments wrong and kick his sorry ass.
Mon-Fri 1pm-10pm, Sat 10am-10pm, Sun 10am-9pm. £12 for 30 laps, £17 for 50.

www.itchy**sheffield**.co.uk   71 ☐

■ ■ Foundry Climbing Centre

Unit 2, 45 Mowbray Street (0114) 279 6331

Pretend you're on Gladiators and scale the 13 metre high walls, with top rope climbs and 150 routes. Full instruction is available and there are walls suitable for beginners through to the more advanced climber.

Adults £5.30 week, £5.50 W/E, Conc. £3.50, Children £3
Mon-Fri 10am-10pm, Sat/Sun 10am-8pm.

■ ■ Owlerton Dog Racing

Owlerton Stadium (0114) 234 3074

It's cheap to get in (cheaper if you get there later), tasty pork sandwiches on offer and many dogs with humorous names for you to bet your 50p on. A cracking night out.

Open 7.30pm-11pm. Tue £2, Fri/Sat £4.50.

■ ■ Paintball Commando

Wakefield (01924) 242 1330

www.monster.co.uk is an excellent recruitment website covering all your employment needs. Whether it be career guidance, tips on improving your interview technique, or just frank and clear advice when you find yourself suddenly unemployed following a mock execution of your boss with a paint gun in a field in Wakefield.

£15pp/day. Refreshments, equipment, over-alls and facemask inc. £7 per 100 paint pots.

■ ■ Sheffield Ski Village

4 Vale Road (0114) 276 9459

Not quite as sunny as the French Alps but with all the falling over fun of going down a hill really quickly on two long planks, means it's so good you'll soon think it's Val D'Isere rather than Vale Road.

£16.95 for 90 minutes. Mon-Sun 9am-10pm.

■ ■ Casino

■ ■ Grosvenor Casino

Queens Road (0114) 275 7433

Black jack and roulette. Food served 'til late.

Open everyday 2pm-4am. Free membership.

■ ■ Museums and Galleries

■ ■ The City Museum

Weston Park (0114) 278 2600

Set in the beautiful grounds of Weston Park, the impressive exterior of the City Museum is spoiled somewhat once you venture inside. Fossils, evolution wall charts and old coins don't really do it for me any more. There are a couple of saving graces though – there's a lovingly put together room of Sheffield Wednesday photos and memorabilia, pride of place being given to the sheepskin coat of commentator John Motson.

Tue-Sat 10am-5pm, Sun 11am-5pm. Free.

■ ■ Graves Art Gallery

Surrey Street (0114) 278 2600

In spite of Sheffield's limited art scene, the good old city council came up trumps with this eight gallery delight spanning the entire third floor of the Central Library. Worthy of more publicity, it's not the flashiest of venues but the work here is of an

IT'S THE MD

exceptional quality, ranging from the etchings of Goya and Piranesi to a comprehensive collection of the changing British Art Movement from 1900-1990. There's also regular extensive photography exhibitions.
Mon-Sat 10am-5pm. Closed Sun
Free admission.

■ ■ ■ Mappin Art Gallery
Weston Park (0114) 278 2600

Connected to the City Museum which, in startling contrast to the Graves, is a pleasant airy environment to potter round on a lazy Sunday afternoon. Space is limited with only four rooms, two for permanent works (British and European paintings from 16th to 19th century), and the larger two for visiting exhibitions. It's these that add the interest to the gallery, with the focus on symbolic and experimental work, particularly sculpture.
Tue-Sat 10am-5pm, Sun 11am-5pm
Free admission.

■ ■ ■ Millennium Galleries
Arundel Gate (0114) 278 2600

Sheffield's answer to The Tate Modern, one floor in this huge building is devoted to exhibits, and the two permanent features are the staid "metalwork" and "craft and design". The temporary touring exhibits are the main focus, and as they are on loan they contain works you may not get to see without otherwise taking a long trip or two.
Mon-Sat 10am-5pm (open till 9pm Wed), Sun 11am-5pm
Free (charge for temporary exhibits).

■ ■ ■ Site Gallery
1 Brown Street (0114) 281 2077

Small, but well-used exhibition space dedicated to photographic and visual media works, (makes a stimulating and interesting change from the normal still life, bowl of fruit fare on offer elsewhere). There's a groovy little café next door and facilities such as darkrooms and digital imaging are available for hire upstairs, so you can develop and manipulate all those piccies that Boots won't.
Tue-Fri 11pm-6pm, Sat 11am-5.30pm, Sun 1pm-5pm, Free admission.

■ ■ ■ Days Out

■ ■ ■ Bishops House
Norton Leeds Lane (0114) 278 2600

Hidden away at the top of Meers Brook Park, this place was built in the 1500s and is the oldest surviving timber frame house in Sheffield. It contains many of its original fea

SHOW HIM YOU'RE NOT INTIMIDATED

tures which give you a glimpse of what England was like in Tudor and Stewart times. Its elevated location also provides panoramic views of the city which are pretty impressive.
Sat 10am-4.30pm, Sun 11am-4.30pm.
Free admission.

▉ ▉ ▉ Botanical Gardens
Clarkehouse Road (0114) 250 0500

Picnics, frisbee, footy, canoodling, whatever takes your fancy, the Botanical Gardens are perfect for those plentiful sunny days in Sheffield. Presently undergoing a £6.7 million renovation, it's one of Sheffield's few 'green' areas. Watch out for the bear pit – it's cool, if you can find it.

▉ ▉ ▉ Chatsworth House
Bakewell, Derbyshire (01246) 565300
Set in the heart of the Peak District, covering 105 acres, Chatsworth House is an impressive and lavish stately home. The gardens can be visited separately, and make the perfect picnic location. The house boasts a collection of paintings by Rembrandt and Gainsborough.
Opens 11am, last admission 4.30pm.
House & Gardens, Adults £7, NUS £5.75, Children £3.

▉ ▉ ▉ Peak District
A short car journey out to the west of Sheffield brings you to the Peak District. Here you'll find some of Britain's most spectacular countryside. If you're feeling energetic you can take a walk amongst the hills or you can drive around at leisure visiting the likes of Matlock, Bakewell and Castleton. In Matlock you can take a cable car ride up to the Heights of Abraham, a vantage point with stunning views over the valley. In Bakewell you can try the local delicacy, the Bakewell Tart and wander through the pretty streets. For the more adventurous there are caverns galore in Castleton and numerous quaint little pubs to quieten your nerves before you enter the underground depths.

▉ ▉ ▉ Tropical Butterfly House and Wildlife Centre
Hungerhill Farm, Woodsetts Road, North Anston (01909) 569 416
Butterfly house, meadows and gardens for young children to run through shrieking with excitement. There's also the opportunity to hold one of their "exotic" animals, which reminds me of a film I once saw, but that's a different story.
£3.50 adults, £2.50 children, £2.75 conc.

JUST KEEP SMILING AT HIM

■■■ Days Out of the City

If you really want to use that sandcastle equipment you can take the trip to the seaside for the day, with a choice of **Whitby**, **Filey** or sunny **Scarborough**. **Scarborough** is the largest of the three and as a result has three times as many kiss-me-quick hats. If you'd like to learn a little bit more about the creatures on the beach visit the **Sea Life Centre**, which as well as having over 30 displays of brightly coloured fish, also houses a seal rescue centre. There's also the **Atlantis** water park, or pop on one of the many guided tours and learn a little more about the history of the city.

If you're more of a city type and want to shop 'til you drop head towards nearby **Manchester** or **Leeds**. Both have a bevy of cool bars and shops to fritter your money away in. For the more cultural amongst you try **The Lowry** in Salford, Manchester, alternatively **The City Art Gallery** or **Henry Moore Institute** in Leeds. If it's shops you're

after Manchester has the infamous **King Street** with its designer boutiques, and price tags, **Kendals** or the soon to be open **Harvey Nichols**. Speaking of which, max that card at the one in Leeds or peruse **The Victoria Quarter** for that something special. As far as bars go you can't get any funkier than those on Manchester's **Oldham Street** or in the **Castlefield** area. Leeds fights back with the groovy **Call Lane** area. Pick up **itchy Manchester** or **itchy Leeds** for more info (0113 246 0440).

If you long for the fresh air of the countryside take an invigorating trip to the **Peak District**, a short car or train journey west of Sheffield. **Hope Valley**, **Matlock** and **Eyam** are the nearest areas to Sheffield, but it's all pretty accessible, so if you fancy the confectionery delights of **Bakewell**, or the bubbling springs of **Buxton** you won't have far to travel. If you fancy something a little bit racier throw caution to the wind and visit one of the local theme parks, such as **Lightwater Valley**. Although requiring a bit of a drive to get there, it's well worth it, for loads of scary and exciting rides that will make you lose your lunch.

■■ Sport

■■ Sheffield Eagles
Don Valley Stadium (0114) 261 0326
A relatively young rugby club, the Eagles were formed in 1982 and have quickly become a team to be reckoned with. There's a buzzing atmosphere at their games, as long as you don't mind loads of aggressive Yorkshire men bawling their lungs out shouting "kick it yer big girl". It's a cracking experience, and with plenty of South Yorkshire teams around, there's often a regular grudge match for you to get your teeth into.
Tickets £9.

■■ Sheffield Sharks
**Sheffield Arena, Broughton Lane
(0114) 256 5656**
It's well worth the trek down to Broughton Lane. Winners of the 2001 BBL Northern Conference and The Rose Bowl Trophy, the Sharks' predatory pursuit of the top honours

looks likely to continue well into the 2002 season. From a marginal team a few seasons ago, the Sharks now turn out to play in front of packed houses. Fast, frenetic and they sell hotdogs.
Adults £8 Students/U.15's £5.

■■ Sheffield Steelers
**Sheffield Arena, Broughton Lane
(0114) 240 0088**
One of the swiftest growing spectator sports in the UK. Fast, intense, extremely entertaining and pretty violent all set in the easily accessible Sheffield Arena. The Steelers have consistently been the most successful club in the UK, and the speed in which they took the 2001 Sekonda ISL Championship is testament to their icy dominance. This is one of the few sports where a Sheffield side really excels, and it's absolutely compelling viewing.
Adults £9.50, Students/OAP's £8, Child £6

■■ Sheffield Tigers Speedway
**Owlerton Sports Stadium, Penistone Rd
(0114) 285 3142**
Sheffield's speedway team have had a striking record in recent years, delivering an impressive Premiership treble and continuing to excel in domestic competitions. Their Evil Kinevil antics are made all the more impressive given that they drive incredibly fast bikes with no brakes. Sounds pretty good on paper doesn't it – it's even better when you're there.
*Adults £8.50, Children £4, Family of four £20
Racenight: Thursdays @ 7.45pm.*

■ ■ ■ Sheffield United F.C.
Bramall Lane (0114) 221 5757

The local derby matches twice a year are the highlight of the football calendar, which was almost put paid to last year by United's spectacular nosedive down the 1st Division table in a manner that Jurgen Klinsmann would be proud of. The beginning of each season always heralds a new dawn for the Blades, which they've often failed to live up to. This time round, as always, their huge brigade of faithful followers will be hoping for big things. With a new investment in youth, and a bit more stability being brought to the club, the future looks promising for the Blades.
Adults £10-£18, Concessions £5-£9.

■ ■ Sheffield Wednesday F.C.
Hillsborough (0114) 221 2121/221 2400
The Owls are one of the oldest clubs in the Football League, with an illustrious past and dedicated, proud supporters; their stadium is an impressive spectacle and one of the foremost grounds in the country. Unfortunately the team aren't anywhere near as spectacular. After relegation from the Premiership in the 99/2000 season, the Owls even slumped as far down as bottom of the 1st before dragging themselves clear of the relegation zone. The influx of foreign players that created a cosmopolitan feel to the place have slowly been weeded out. They obviously realised that although Wednesday's kit may look a bit like Internationale's, that's where the similarity ends.
Adults £14-£20, Concessions £9-£11.

Holly, 21, Barmaid

When you're not pulling pints where do you have pints pulled for you?
Revolution & Forum Café
And where do you eat young lady?
BB's
Favourite club in Sheffield? Bed
And where do you get dressed for Bed? Ark, Alley, Versa Women
What's the best thing about Sheffield?
There are some great clubs
And the worst?
Hardly any late bars

BiLASH *Tandoori* HOUSE 0114 266 1746
www.bilasht.tandoori.co.uk
vegetarian takeaway menu

◼◼◼ Hairdressers

◼◼◼ 284 Hair
284 Ecclesall Road (0114) 266 4045
Women's cut and blow from £16.50, Men's from £10
Mon-Thu 9-5, Fri 9-7, Sat 9-4

◼◼◼ Alan Paul
5 Park Lane, Meadowhall (0114) 256 8662
Women from £24, Men from £18
Mon-Fri 10-9, Sat 9-7, Sun 11-5

◼◼◼ Avanti
303 Ecclesall Road (0114) 267 9119
Women from £23, Men from £16
20% discount for students
Mon-Wed 10-5.30, Thu-Fri 10-8, Sat 9.30-4.30

◼◼◼ Capelli Hair
81 Junction Road, Hunters Bar (0114) 268 2691
Women and Men from £15
Mon-Tue 9.30-5, Wed 9.30-6.45, Thu 9.30-7, Fri 9.30-5.45, Sat 9-4.30

◼◼◼ Etienne
23 Division Street (0114) 276 3132
Women from £20, Men from £17
Mon-Wed 9-6, Thu-Fri 9-7, Sat 9-6

◼◼◼ Halo
106 Devonshire Street (0114) 272 9799
Women from £24, Men from £15
Mon-Tue 10-6, Wed-Fri 10-8, Sat 9-6

◼◼◼ La Coupe Salon
54-56 Fargate (0114) 275 0505
Women from £22.50, Men from £12.50

body
www.itchysheffield.co.uk

50% discount for students
Mon-Tue 10-5, Wed-Thu 10-7, Fri 9-7, Sat 9-5

■■■ Sweeney 4
290 Ecclesall Road (0114) 264 0474
Women from £16.95, Men from £9.95
20% discount for students
Mon-Fri 9-8, Sat 9-5.30

■■■ Taylor, Taylor
Men's salon 47 Surrey Street
(0114) 272 1837
From £11.90
Mon-Fri 8.30-5.15, Sat 8.30-3.30
Women's salon 37 Surrey Street
(0114) 272 3351
From £24.95
Mon-Wed 9-5.30, Thu-Fri 9-7, Sat 8.30-3.30

■■■ Toni and Guy
52 Pinstone Street
(0114) 275 7770
Women from £26, Men from £20
Mon-Thu 9.30-5.30, Fri 9.30-7, Sat 8.45-4.30

■■■ XM Hair
206 West Street (0114) 272 5500
Women from £23, Men from £13
Mon-Thu 9-5, Fri 9-7, Sat 9-4

■■■ Beauty Salons

■■■ Lynda V Price
772-774 Ecclesall Road (0114) 268 3093
Manicures, pedicures, massage, facials and
electrolysis
Manicure £9.95
Mon 9.30-8, Tue-Fri 10-7.30, Sat 9-3.30

■■■ The Retreat
750 Ecclesall Road (0114) 266 6559
Semi-permanent cosmetics, tattoos, waxing,
non-surgical facelifts, manicures, nail exten-
sions and facials, 10% discount for students.
Manicure £15
*Mon 9.30-5.30, Tue10-6, Wed-Thu 9.30-8,
Fri 9.30-6, Sat 9-4*

■■■ Ranmoor Beauty Clinic
366 Fulwood Road (0114) 230 9192
Full beauty treatments including manicures
and facials.
Manicure £7.50
Tue 9.30-5.30, Wed 9.30-8, Thu-Fri 9-6, Sat 9-2

■■■ Health Clubs and Gyms

■■■ Body and Soul
YMCA Sheff Hallam Uni (0114) 268 4807
Fitness studio, sports hall, steam room
and sauna.
Membership £299 for peak times.
Mon-Fri 7-10, Sat 9-6, Sun 9-4

■■■ Ladies Executive Health Club
Lescar Building, Lescar Lane
(0114) 267 9379
Gym, sunbed, sauna and aerobics classes.
Membership £20.
Mon-Sat 9am-10pm

■ ■ ■ Ponds Forge International Sports Centre
Sheaf Street (0114) 279 9766

Everything about it screams big, expensive and athletic – as an international sports venue it attracts athletes from all over the country. If you can brave your way past the super-slim, super-toned, super-tanned freaks that congregate round the reception area, you'll find that membership is surprisingly good value for money. You pay nothing to join and for a small monthly fee you get free access to two multi-gyms, Olympic and leisure pools, fitness classes and the health suite. The upstairs gym is more geared to pound shedding than posing, but why go to the gym when you can saunter off for a nice sauna?

■ ■ ■ Fringe Health & Fitness Club
94 Surrey Street (0114) 275 3755
Sauna, jacuzzi, hair and beauty salon and full gym.
Membership £26 per month.
Student discounts.
Mon-Fri 7-9.30, Sat 9-6, Sun 9-3

■ ■ ■ West Street Workout
52 West Street (0114) 273 9074
Cardiovascular and aerobic gym facilities. Early bird membership £75, off peak £130, peak £185.
Mon-Thu 7.30am-8pm, Fri 7.30-7, Sat 10-2, Sun 11-2

■ ■ Tattoo Parlours

■ ■ ■ Body art
337 Glossop Road (0114) 275 8804
Prices vary, *Mon-Sat 10-6*

■ ■ ■ Body Poppers
Forum, Devonshire Street (0114) 275 4333
Piercing from £10, *Mon-Sat 10-6*

■ ■ ■ Eternal Ink & Primal Piercing
272 Glossop Road (0113) 249 3843
Tattoos from £20, *Thu-Mon 12-6*

■ ■ ■ Feline
8 Hickmott Road (0114) 266 1817
Mon-Sat 10-6

■ ■ ■ Steel City Tattooing
88 London Road (0114) 276 0550
From £5, *Mon-Sat 10-5*

itchy cities...

Glasgow

Edinburgh

Leeds

York

Manchester

Liverpool

Sheffield

Nottingham

Birmingham

Cambridge

Cardiff

Oxford

Bristol

London

Bath

Brighton

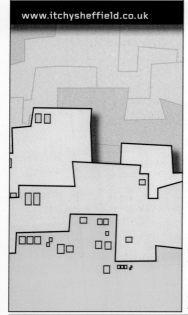

■ ■ Pizzas, Burgers & Kebabs

■ ■ Burger King
Highgate (0114) 275 6164
Mon-Thu 9am-9pm, Fri-Sat 9am-11pm,
Sun 10am-9pm

■ ■ Chick King
233 London Rd (0114) 258 1341
Mon-Sun 6pm-12am

■ ■ Domino's Pizza
886 Ecclesall Rd (0114) 266 9988
Mon-Thu 4pm-12am, Fri-Sat 12pm-1am,
Sun 12pm-12am, Free home delivery.

■ ■ Kebab House
517 Abbeydale Rd (0114) 255 5442
Mon-Sat 6pm-3am, Sun 5pm-1am

■ ■ McDonald's
1-5 The Moor (0114) 273 1621
Mon-Thu 7.30am-12am,
Fri-Sat 7.30am-2am, Sun 7.30am-11am
10-12 High St (0114) 275 2605
Mon-Sun 7am-12am

■ ■ Nibbles Pizza
465 Glossop Rd (0114) 268 2529
Mon-Sun 5pm-12am
Free delivery for orders over £8.

■ ■ Millennium Takeaway
205 Whitham Rd, B/hill (0114) 267 8822
Mon-Sun 11am-1am.
Free delivery within a 4 mile radius.

■ ■ Perfect Pizza
294 Prince of Wales Rd (0114) 265 0007
Mon-Sun 4pm-12am, Free delivery.

Torino's
235 London Rd (0114) 258 5400
Mon-Thu 5pm-1.30am, Fri-Sat 5pm-3am
Free delivery within a 3 mile radius.

Indian/Asian

Balti King
216 Fulwood Rd (0114) 266 6655
Mon-Sun 10am-3am
Free delivery (after 5.30pm – 4 mile radius).

Bilash Tandoori House Indian Takeaway
347 Sharrow Vale Rd (0114) 266 1746

Award winning Indian on Sharrow Vale Road that offers a huge array of inviting dishes from tantalising tandooris to delicious dopi-azas. They've been going strong since 1986, and many of the locals know to seek out this place when looking for some top Indian grub. There's also an extensive vegetarian menu which is arguably the best in Sheffield. Demands a visit tonight.
Sun-Thu 5.30pm-12am, Fri-Sat 5.30pm-1am

Hamid's Balti House
983 Ecclesall Rd (0114) 266 0155
Mon-Sun 5.30pm-11.30pm

Takdir Indian Takeaway
339 Ecclesall Rd South (0114) 262 1818
Mon-Sun 5pm-10.30pm. Home delivery.

Oriental

Chinos
19 London Rd (0114) 273 7777
Mon-Thu 5pm-3am, Fri-Sat 5pm-4am,
Sun 5pm-12am

Living Spring
4 Hickmott Rd (0114) 268 6883
Sun 7pm-12am, Mon-Sat 6pm-12am

Wok This Way
394 Fulwood Rd (0114) 230 3008
Mon-Sun 4.30pm-11.45pm,

Fish & Chips

A Salt 'N' Battered
111 London Rd (0114) 258 4835
Mon-Thu 4.45pm-7pm, Fri 4pm-12am,
Sat4.45pm-7pm

Banner Cross Fish Bar
989 Ecclesall Rd (0114) 267 8333
Tue-Fri 10am-1.30am, Sat 11.30am-2am

Broomhill Friery
197 Whitham Rd (0114) 266 2802
Mon-Sat 4.30pm-12pm

The Grand Potato
577 Abbeydale Rd (0114) 249 5014
Mon-Sun 5.30pm-11.45pm

BiLASH Tandoori HOUSE 0114 266 1746 www.bilashtandoori.co.uk Indian takeaway

useful info

www.itchysheffield.co.uk

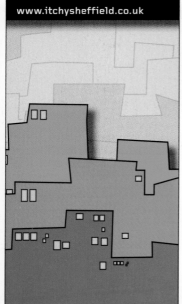

■■■ Travel

■■■ Taxis/Private Hire

Abbey Taxis	(0114) 275 1111
Alpha Taxis	(0114) 232 1321
Central Cab Co	(0114) 276 9869
Ace Cars	(0114) 273 7475
Airport Express UK	(0114) 255 5656
City Cars	(0114) 265 1651
Dial-A-Cab	0800 244 442
Fleet Car	(0114) 258 5858

■■■ Buses

First Mainline (local)	(0114) 256 7000
National Express	08705 808080
Stagecoach Supertram	(0114) 272 8282

■■■ Trains

National Rail Enquiries	08457 484950
Central Trains	0345 056 027
Midland Mainline	0345 221 125
Network (local trains)	(01709) 515 151
Virgin Train	08457 222 333

■■■ Car Hire

Avis Rent a Car	(0114) 272 8981
Budget	(0114) 275 5377

itchy**sheffield** 2002

There's **better things** to spend **money** on.

Don't waste it on travel.

If you're under 26 or a student save £££'s on travel with a Young Persons' Discount Coachcard. Cards cost £9 and save you up to 30% off already low fares all year. Register online to receive special offers throughout the year.

For journey planning, tickets and coachcards

visit **GoByCoach.com** or call 08705 80 80 80

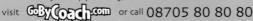

Check online for details.
Coach services depart from Interchange, Sheffield.

■ ■ Accommodation

Prices are for a double and brekkie unless we say otherwise. Prices tend to vary – if you ring and beg you can often get a better price.

■ ■ Expensive

■ ■ Hilton Sheffield Hotel
Victoria Quays (0114) 252 5500
Week : £140 W/E: £78

■ ■ Mid-priced

■ ■ Hotel Bristol
Blonk Street (0114) 220 4000

The most impressive Sheffield city centre hotel, but happily not the most expensive. The plush, stylish and comfortable rooms, plus a relaxed and informal atmosphere make this a great place to stay. Most of the rooms are spacious and include a sofa bed so your mate can crash there when you pull at 'Crasher.
Week: £54. 49 W/E: £49.50
Full English Bkfast £8.50 Continental £6.95

■ ■ Ibis
Shude Hill (0114) 241 9600
£42 at all times. Breakfast extra.

■ ■ Nether Edge Hotel
Montgomery Road (0114) 255 4363
£40 at all times.

■ ■ Novotel
50 Arundel Gate (0114) 278 1781
Week: £79 W/E: £69.75
Breakfast extra Mon-Fri but inc. at weekends.

■ ■ The Rutland Hotel
452 Glossop Road (0114) 266 4411
Week: £75 W/E: £68.50. Breakfast extra.

■ ■ Swallow Hotel
Kenwood Road (0114) 258 3811
Week: £95 W/E: £70. Breakfast extra.

■■ Budget

■■ Riverside Court Hotel

2-10 Nursery Street (0114) 273 1962
£39 at all time. Breakfast £3.50.

■■ The Lindum Hotel

90 Montgomery Rd (0114) 255 2356
Week: £30 W/E: £33

■■ St. Pellegrino

Oak Park (0114) 268 1953
£26 single at all times.

■■ Student Accommodation

■■ Victoria Hall

Eldon Street (0114) 289 3500

I miss being a student, not only are they the best years of your life sodden in remarkably cheap beer, but at this place you'll enjoy some of the best accommodation that you're likely to experience throughout most of your 20s. At Victoria Hall you'll find brand spanking new student housing. The flats are fully furnished, there's a shower and toilet in each room, Sky TV in each flat, 24-hour manned security and CCTV, plus a fully equipped kitchen. Gone are the days where your parents worry about you roughing it in some dingy digs, now they're just wondering why your new place is nicer than back at home?

■■ Media

■■ Entertainment & Listings

www.itchysheffield.co.uk – the insider guide for all things entertainment and by far and away the best damn site on the shonky world wide web (no bias there then). Carries daily updated articles, venue and event listings information.

www.sheffieldscene.co.uk – reasonable site covering venues in Sheffield. Updated twice a decade, so the information can be a bit unreliable.

www.steellounge.co.uk – pretty good site covering bars and clubs in Sheffield.

■■ Radio

■■ BBC Radio Sheffield

54 Shoreham Street (0114) 273 1177
Frequency: 88.6 FM
Cat stuck up a tree? Tram to Meadowhall two minutes late? Hear about it here first. Conservative music policy, but quite popular for work-experience with local students.

■ ■ Galaxy
15 Paternoster Row (0114) 221 0500
Frequency:105 FM

Covers Sheffield, Leeds and York, with a music policy orientated around chart and dance. Also that fox from the Boddingtons adverts, Melanie Sykes, does a show on Saturdays.

■ ■ Hallam FM
900 Herries Road (0114) 285 3333
Frequency:102.9FM

Pretty good local radio station knocking out choons to the Attercliffe massif. Mainstream chart hits, and dance at the weekends.

■ ■ Newspapers

■ ■ Barnsley Chronicle
47 Church Street (01226) 734734

Want to know what's happening in Barnsley? Thought not, but in the event that you do, check out this local paper. Released Fridays.

■ ■ The Sheffield Mercury
41 Bromwich Road (0114) 274 6555

Newspaper that covers entertainment and stage events in Sheffield. Free paper distributed in pubs and working mens clubs throughout the city, so you can easily pick up a copy, assuming you're brave enough to go in and get it. Released on Wednesday evenings, this rag will keep you up to date on where Maurice is playing the spoons tonight.

■ ■ Steel Press
University of Sheffield Student Union (0114) 222 2000

Reasonable student newspaper, released fortnightly during term time. Ever worry that University stiffles young writers. I worry that it doesn't stiffle enough of them.

■ ■ Sheffield Star
York Street (0114) 276 7676

Daily newspaper covering everything that's going on in the Steel city. On Saturdays it incorporates the Green'un – a great sports newspaper that'll keep you up to date on Wednesday's latest thrashing at home.

■ ■ Sheffield Telegraph
York Street (0114) 275 4896

Weekly newspaper covering all things Sheff. You'd have thought that they'd find enough material to bring it out daily – just lazy I suppose. Released Fridays.

■ ■ Yorkshire Evening Post
Wellington Street, Leeds (0113) 243 2701

Daily newspaper carrying local and national stories. Large sections on jobs and accommodation.

■ ■ Yorkshire Post
Wellington Street, Leeds (0113) 243 2701

As above, but it comes out earlier in the day, and looks more like a broadsheet newspaper.

top 5...
Outdoor Drinking

1. The Fat Cat
2. The Lescar
3. Yorkshire Grey
4. Nursery Tavern
5. The Porter Brook

www.itchysheffield.co.uk

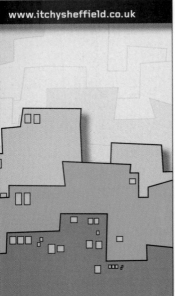

■■ Drinking

Extend the drinking fun at **The Halcyon** bar or **The Forum Café** which are open 'til 1am Mon-Sat, closing for church on Sunday. **The Showroom bar** is open 'til 1am on Fridays and Saturdays. **Brown Street** opposite is open 'til 2am all week, apart from Tuesdays and Sundays.

■■ Cigarettes

BP Express on the Ring Road, the filling station on Greenland Road and Darnell are open 24 hours, as is the **Elf** on Sheffield Road, Tinsley, the **Shell** on Handsworth Road and that lovely **Texaco** on Burley Moor Road.

■■ Late Supermarkets

Asda on Market Street generally closes at 8 or 9pm (except on Sundays when the opening hours are 10-4), but on Thursdays and Fridays it stays open 'til 10pm. **Tesco** at 685 Chesterfield Rd closes at 8pm on weekdays, but **Sainsburys** on Archer Road is open 'til 10pm on Saturdays, 8pm on Mondays and Tuesdays 'til 9pm, Wednesdays 'til 10pm and on Thursdays and Fridays 'til a staggering midnight.

■■ Late Serving Restaurants

Good old **Pizza Express** does it again, serving 'til midnight every night including Sunday. Unsurprisingly Sheff always has a curry house, or twenty, to tickle your taste buds after a few ales. **Anila's and Vijays** on Charter Square stay open 'til late, **SB's** is open 'til 2.30am during the week and 3am at the weekends, but for the daddy of all curries no one can hold a candle to **Balti King** in Broomhill. The King is open 'til 4am every night knocking out some of the best baltis in the city.

■ ■ Post Club Action

Niche springs to the rescue at the weekends, pumping out uplifting house and garage 'til noon the next day. At **Mojo's** the Insomniacz crew play hard house 'til noon. There also tends to be after show parties at **The Halcyon** or **The Forum Café**, but often you just have to see how things go on the night – so keep your eyes open – although they really should be shut at this time of night.

■ ■ Late Night Shopping

Forgotten your sibling's birthday gift and need to stop off on the way to their birthday meal? Have no fear, the glorious **Meadowhall** shopping centre is open 'til 9pm every weekday night and 'til 7pm on Saturdays (only open 11-5pm Sundays.) So if your boss won't let you shop in your lunch hour all is not lost.

■ ■ After Work Beauty Fix

Avanti is open 'til 8pm on Thursdays and Fridays, **284 Hair** 'til 7pm on Friday, and both **Halo** and **Hairband** carry on cutting 'til 8pm Wed-Fri. But for shear staying power both **Alan Paul** and **Sweeney 4** are open 'til 8pm every weeknight – so you have no excuse for not looking perfectly coiffed all the time. If it's your face that needs a little bit of work **The Retreat** beauty salon on Ecclesall Road has late nights on Wednesdays and Thursdays 'til 8pm, and offers a full range of services from facials and tanning to the more exotic seaweed body wrap. If you fancy something a little more spiritual, **Beauty Works** on Crookes Road, offers Reiki, and nails and stuff, 'til 7pm on Tuesdays and Thursdays.

■ ■ Late Night Culture

There are certain venues that are always open for after work activities. If you want to catch a late movie head to **The Showroom**, **UGC**, **UCI** or **Warner Village**, with last showings at around 10pm, and midnight at weekends. If you don't really see Steven Segal's latest offering as a 'cultural' one, then the **Millennium Galleries** is open 'til 9pm on a Wednesday, and Sheffield theatres, **The Lyceum** or **The Crucible**, have performances starting at around 7.30/8pm every night.

■ ■ Other Places

Grosvenor Casino is open everyday from 2pm 'til 4am or gambling of another kind occurs at **Owlerton Stadium**, which holds evening greyhound races between 6 and 10pm, but take your coat it's parky out there.

■ NIGHTMARES ON WAX • COM

calling all writers

We're looking for writers for itchysheffield.co.uk. Experts who know their stuff across every area – music, clubs, restaurants, bars, the arts – the whole shebang. Whatever your speciality, if you'd like to get involved, then send us an email to **sheffieldwriters@itchymedia.co.uk** with a sample of either a venue review or something entertaining you've written, and we'll have a read through and get in touch.